Patriots, Pirates, and Pineys

Sixty Who Shaped New Jersey

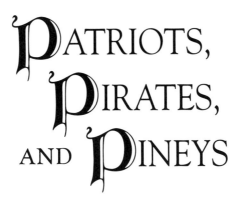

PATRIOTS, PIRATES, AND PINEYS

Sixty Who Shaped New Jersey

ROBERT A. PETERSON

Plexus Publishing, Inc.
Medford, New Jersey

Copyright© 1998 Robert A. Peterson

Published by: Plexus Publishing, Inc.
143 Old Marlton Pike
Medford, NJ 08055

Library of Congress Cataloging-in-Publication Data

Peterson, Robert A.
   Patriots, Pirates, and Pineys: Sixty Who Shaped New Jersey /
by Robert A. Peterson.
      p.   cm.
   ISBN 0-937548-37-5 (hard). -- ISBN 0-937548-39-1 (soft)
   1. New Jersey--Biography.   I. Title.
CT249.P48   1998
   920.0749--dc21   98-15153
                                                                  CIP

Printed in the United States of America.

Price: $29.95 (hardcover); $19.95 (softcover)

Editor: Rhonda Forbes
Cover Design: Bette Tumasz and Jacqueline Walter

CONTENTS

ᴀCKNOWLEDGEMENTS

Because this book is about the area in which I was born and raised, there are hundreds of people to whom I owe a debt of gratitude. My extended family—Clarence Peterson, Walter Henschel, Edmund Einsiedel, and their children and grandchildren—all stimulated my interest, first in family history, and then American history with their stories and values from the past.

From my elementary teachers in Egg Harbor schools I heard tales of Cornelius Mey, Batsto, and the American Revolution in story circles at the old Lafayette Firehouse Library. Local history buffs—Paul Kroekel, George Baulig, Ron Hesse, Ethel Roesch, and others—gave me many insights on the "olden days." My readers—people who have faithfully read my column, "Our South Jersey Heritage," in *The Hammonton News*, *Egg Harbor News*, or other local weekly—are the best! By supporting my column, they've given me the opportunity to continue extensive research on local history. Because of them, every 7 days I must research another topic, write another column. My readers' insights, correspondence, corrections, and stories have deepened my knowledge and appreciation of South Jersey and its people.

Many other writers have been my tutors through their books, especially William McMahon, whom I consider the "Dean of South Jersey Historians." Jo Kapus, Craig Koedel, Budd Wilson, and Antoinette Doell were all helpful through either their books or insights.

I would also like to thank my newspaper editor, Norlynne Lubrano, for her support of my work, as well as the entire *Vineland Times–Graphics* organization. Many of these chapters first appeared in one form or another in *The Egg Harbor News*, *Hammonton News*, *Atlantic County Record*, or *Mainland Journal*. The Egg Harbor Historical Society, the Hammonton Historical Society, the Vineland Historical Society, the Cape May Historical Society, and The Pilgrim Academy Library under the able direction of Elizabeth Surpless have all been of great help over the years. Special thanks go to Lois Boone of Seneca, South Carolina, my assistant of many years who typed the first draft.

The Pilgrim Academy organization has provided a wonderful atmosphere in which to work, since the school encourages its faculty to engage in research, writing, and public service. My administrative assistant, Mary Adkisson, deserves special praise for the efficiency with which she runs our office, giving me time to think and reflect on history, philosophy, and education. Rhonda Forbes of Plexus Publishing, Inc., who worked with me on the project, did an excellent job tracking down pictures and illustrations, and deserves much praise.

Finally, I would like to thank Tom Hogan of Plexus Publishing, Inc. for his interest and confidence in the project. In this day of fast-paced business and information technology, it still comes down to personal relationships and people. Tom understands that is what this book is all about.

This book is dedicated to my seven children, Rebecca, Robert III, Joseph, James, David, Priscilla, and Rachel, but most of all, my wife, Susanna. To her, I echo the sentiments that Philip Fithian, one of the heroes in this book, wrote to his wife: "Peace and God's blessings be with you, my dear wife, forever may you be happy." —Robert A. Peterson Jr., Germania, 1998

INTRODUCTION

No region of the nation has a richer heritage than Southern New Jersey. The only problem is that the full story has yet to be told. Virginia has its restored Williamsburg, Texas has its Alamo, and Massachusetts has its Sturbridge Village, and so on. These places are famous and known to us not only because of what happened at each place, but because people and governments have made concerted efforts to preserve the past. South Jerseyans are not like that. For the most part, they'd rather stay out of the limelight. South Jerseyans are too modest to tell you that Betsy Ross lived here, as did Patience Wright, America's first female sculptor; Simon Lake, the inventor of the submarine; and Joseph Napoleon, brother of the French dictator. World famous businesses started here include Welch's Grape Juice, Campbell's Soup, and the whole American glass industry.

This book was written to help address the problem of ignorance about one of America's best-kept secrets—the rich heritage of the Shore and Pine Barrens regions of New Jersey. And there's no better way to learn about the history of any area than through biography.

Not only is it informative, but it's also just plain fun. To find out that Francis Hopkinson, one of the signers of the Declaration of Independence, had a head no bigger than an apple proves the truth of the statement that truth is stranger than fiction. Or that the inventor of America's greatest china was so blind that he could never see his final product. Or that Henry Rowan, the millionaire industrialist, almost lost his childhood business because his mother refused to pay higher prices for his eggs.

But biographies offer more than the fun of incident and anecdote. One begins to discover the illusiveness of a man or a woman's personality, not merely the outer facts of their lives. *The Diary of Isa Leek*, for example, reveals the hardy character of the thousands of women who built this country, helping their husbands' businesses, bearing children, burying their dead, and doing incredible feats of manual work to feed and clothe their families. The love letters written by Philip Fithian to his beloved Laura, on the other hand, show us that young people in love are the same in any generation.

Another joy of reading biographical sketches is that you make new friends. You may not be able to make friends with a neighbor; or perhaps you are living alone. But pick up a copy of *Patriots, Pirates, and Pineys* and you're sure to find someone who is a soul mate. If you are a businessman, you can relate to and even pick up advice from John Wanamaker, who has been dead for 50 years, or Henry Rowan, whose luxuries double as business tools. If you are struggling in business, you can relate to Sara Spenser Washington, who overcame prejudice against African-Americans to establish an international business empire. If you are a woman, you may be inspired by the heroics and humanitarianism of Cornelia Hancock, who nursed the wounded at Gettysburg. If you are a teacher, you'll smile as you read about Antoinette Doell and her experiences in a small town. Of course, meeting new people cuts both ways: With friends like Blackbeard the Pirate or Captain Kidd, you won't need enemies!

There are other friends you will meet. Spend an evening reading about colonial preachers John Brainerd or Charlie Pitman, and you'll be walking shoulder to shoulder with some of the humblest yet strongest men in history. Read about Richard Somers, who gave his life for the new nation on the shores of Tripoli, and you'll be inspired with patriotism for this now well established country of ours.

Many South Jerseyans were acutely aware of their role as patriots. The privateers or private skippers who used their ships to attack the British, and hid in the bays and coves of the intercoastal waterways, were invaluable to the American cause. Samuel Richards of Batsto was cognizant of his role as "Ironmaster to a Nation," especially as he was one of George Washington's chief suppliers of ammunition. John Mathis of what is now Ocean County gave such important help to the patriot cause that official documents of the Continental Congress refer to him as the Great John Mathis. Phillip Vickers Fithian, a minister whose journals were one of the chief sources in the reconstruction of Williamsburg (he served as a tutor there), was one of the leaders of the Jersey Tea Burning at Greenwich, near Bridgeton. He joined up with the Continental Army and gave it moral strength by serving as a chaplain. Meanwhile, sculptress Patience Lovell Wright of Bordentown helped immortalize Washington, Franklin, and other Founding Fathers with her busts of these men. Such reading material, to quote New England minister George Gordon, "Gives one a place in the best society in the world."

Reading about people who made history also helps us to see how others have faced problems and conquered them. Sara Spenser Washington was both black and a woman at a time when few others of either group owned their own businesses, yet she built a business empire. Henry Rowan's two sons died of a rare disease, but he persevered to become a great industrialist and benefactor to thousands of other young people. Captain Henry Sawyer was thrown into the hellhole of a Civil War prison, but he held on to his sanity and health long enough to be honored by Abraham Lincoln.

How people made a living in the past is also inspirational. In New Jersey there are no gold or diamond mines, no oil or coal deposits, no rich farmland like that in Iowa. Yet men like Andrew Rider and women like Elizabeth White found ways to grow and market fruit like the cranberry and blueberry, which grow well in poor, swampy, acidic soil. Caspar Wistar never learned how to blow glass; yet he was able to combine all the factors of production in such a way as to establish the nation's first successful glass factory. Thomas Welch invented Welch's Grape Juice in South Jersey, about the same time that John Campbell was inventing Campbell's Soup near Camden. Henry Hettinger pioneered the airplane in the marshes of South Jersey, while Charles Seabrook pioneered frozen vegetables.

Perhaps the greatest of all joys in reading biographies is of discovering courage in action. And not just from famous people like George Washington or Robert E. Lee, but from people like you and me, from every village and backwater of America, from places like little South Jersey. One can think of courage in sailing unknown waters, as did Erica Mullica and Cornelius Mey. Or courage in founding a town, despite racial prejudice, as did Colonel John McKee. Most histories concentrate on the great rivers of life, the big events. But as historian Will Durant once pointed out, the seemingly unknown people who live on the riverbanks make most of history. These are the stories of people—some famous and some not so famous—who helped make South Jersey, and thus America, what it is today. A few were pirates, some would be called Pineys, but most were patriots. This is their story.

ERICA MULLICA: A RIVER BEARS HIS NAME

Take a trip to the popular Sweetwater Casino Restaurant in Sweetwater, New Jersey, and you'll see the Mullica River much as it looked like when Erica Mullica came here in the early 1600's. The restaurant side is well developed, with docks, boat slips, and houses nearby, but across the river is virgin forest. In many ways, the Mullica River basin must have reminded Mullica of his native Scandinavia, albeit without the mountains. Eventually he would call it home and be the first of many immigrants to the South Jersey pines and coast.

Erica Mullica—who was probably a Finn sailing under the Swedish flag—came to America in 1638 at the age of 15 on either the *Kalmar Nyckel* or the *Fogel Griffin*. Arriving in what is now Salem and Gloucester counties, Mullica lived for awhile in the Swedish settlements at Swedesboro and Raccoon Creek. He married Ingeborg Helm, a sturdy young Swedish girl, whose father was trying to amass a land empire in New Jersey.

For a time, the couple lived in southeastern Pennsylvania. They had six children, of whom at least three lived to become adults—Olof, Eric Jr., and John. But when most men begin to think of retiring—age 61—Mullica was gripped by the wanderlust that had brought him to America when he was just a teenager. And so, he set out to explore the river the Indians called the Amintonck, the river that would later bear his name.

Mullica's ship wasn't the first to enter the mouth of the Amintonck. In the spring of 1614, the Dutch ship *Fortuyn* had ventured into these same waters. Struck by the large numbers of birds' eggs, they dubbed it "Egg Harbor." Then in 1633, another Dutch ship, commanded by David Pieterszen de Vries, sailed into the river. De Vries recorded in his journal that he met with the Indians and saw flocks of birds so large that they darkened the sky. But Mullica apparently explored the river farther inland than any previous explorer. He fell in love with the area.

On the Burlington County side of the river—in what is now Lower Bank—Mullica built a large log cabin (one of Sweden's unique contributions to America) and lived plantation-style on a 100-acre tract of land. Like the plantation owners in Tidewater, Virginia, Mullica depended on the river for travel, communications, and commerce. He was the only white settler to live within 25 miles of what is now Atlantic City. He was the first "Piney."

Mullica made one more move during his lifetime—back to the area of the original Swedish settlements along the Delaware. Here his sons founded Mullica Hill. His Lower Bank property was sold to Joseph Pearce.

Historians have not only had a difficult time keeping track of Mullica's wanderings but of the many spellings of his name as well. Records show variations such as Molica, Mullicus, and Mollicas. We even have a record that says the spelling was Erikka Mullika. The explanation for this is fairly simple. His name in Scandinavian (either Swedish or Finnish) was probably Erikka Mullika. When he reached America, over the years it became Anglicized to Mullica. Variations came because there were no set rules for spelling; people spelled phonetically. If it sounded right, it was spelled right. Set rules didn't come in until the late 1700s with the first dictionaries. The name "Mullicus" came from the custom of Latinizing one's name.

Mullica died in 1723 in Gloucester Township at the ripe old age of 100. He is supposedly buried in the graveyard of Trinity Episcopal Church in Swedesboro. But his name and spirit live on in the beautiful, still relatively wild and undeveloped Mullica River.

CORNELIUS JACOBSEN MEY:
HIS NAME GRACES THE JERSEY CAPE

The Dutch have taken it on the chin for a long time. Ever since the English nearly lost the Anglo-Dutch War in the 1600s, our language has been laced with anti-Dutch expressions.

A "Dutch bargain" is a cheat, while a "Dutch concert" is a musical horror. When someone takes you out, but you wind up paying for the meal, it's a "Dutch treat." And when someone speaks with disagreeable frankness, we say he spoke "Dutch uncle."

The Dutch deserve better. After all, the Dutch have given many things to America: Easter eggs, Santa Claus, waffles, sleighing, skating, and a host of "vans" and "velts" who helped build our nation. And, significantly for New Jersey, it was a Dutchman—Captain Cornelius Jacobsen Mey—who explored and gave his name to Cape May.

Cornelius Mey first came to America as a navigator on the *Fortuyn* (*Fortune*), which hailed from Hoorn, a port in Northern Holland. After making a few landfalls, it headed for home.

Entranced by the mysterious New World, Mey signed on with the Dutch West India Company, which had been given control of New Jersey, to lead an expedition of three ships. Mey sailed in the flagship, the *Blyde Broadschap* (*Glad Tidings*) filled with provisions, articles for trade, and high hopes. After all, another Dutchman, Peter Minuet, had just bought Manhattan Island for $24! Mey had also been granted the title of "First Director of New Netherlands."

Mey reached Manhattan Island in May 1623, then proceeded down the coast, just as Henry Hudson had 14 years earlier. While surveying the coast, Mey fought two battles with the French, who were seeking to carve out their own empire in the New World. Mey defeated the French both times, the second time successfully defending the South River (Delaware) and the "Zuyt Baai" (Delaware Bay).

While on this voyage, Mey gave his name to many different areas. New York Bay he called "Port Mey"; the Delaware he named "New Port Mey"; Cape May was dubbed "Cape Mey"; and South Cape May was named "Cape Cornelius."

3

Across the bay, he named Cape Henlopen after his hometown in Holland. It was a good strategy to have so many places named after himself, for at least one has remained: Cape May. (Through time, the "e" was changed to an "a.")

Mey also helped found a Dutch settlement, Fort Nassau, a few miles south of present-day Camden. Back to Holland and to the director of his company he sent the message that he had discovered "certain new populous and fruitful lands along Zuydt Riviere."

Captain Mey went on to explore the Atlantic Coast as far north as Cape Cod, where he may have even seen the smoke from the Pilgrims' chimneys.

As first Director-General of New Netherlands, Mey established a reputation as an excellent administrator. His superiors in Holland had told him that "Tis better to govern by love and friendship than by force," and the historical record indicates that he followed their good advice, to "the great contentment of his people." He promoted good relations with the Indians, who "came and traded with all the freedom imaginable." When visiting Manhattan and finding that the settlers had a shortage of food and clothes, he supplied them from his ship.

In the mid 1620s Mey returned to Holland, and little is heard about him again in the historical records. Today, however, his name is an important part of our American heritage, as Cape May was America's first seaside resort.

The Dutch push into America in the 17th century was part of a greater flowering of Dutch culture. Newly freed from their Spanish overlords, the Dutch built one of the world's great civilizations. In commerce, Dutch ships plied the Tasman and Bering seas (both named for Dutchmen) and explored so far north that Shakespeare spoke of "ice hanging on a Dutchman's beard." In art, it was the age of Hals, Vermeer, and Rembrandt, while in science it was the age of Huygens and van Leeuwenhoek. By 1625, Holland was engaged in more shipping than all other countries of the world combined. Finally, it was the age of Captain Cornelius Jacobsen Mey, whose name now graces the Jersey Cape.

Henry Jacobs Falkinburg:
Pioneer and Indian Interpreter

In the epic stories of America's westward movement, there are tales of great mountain-men and trailblazers like Jim Bridger and James P. Beckwourth. But before these men could do their work, others had to go before them. Before Colorado could be explored, the Midwest had to be crossed; before the Midwest could be settled, Pennsylvania had to be breached; and before Pennsylvania could be explored, New Jersey had to be opened up. In the 1600s one of the men who did just that was Henry Jacobs Falkinburg.

Henry Jacobs Falkinburg was originally from Holstein, a German province next to Denmark. In those days, nation-states were still forming and he apparently moved between the Protestant states of Holstein, Denmark, and Holland. He probably came to the New World with the Dutch, those hardy explorers who gave us place names like Barnegat, Haarlem, Cape Mey, and Hoboken. When Peter Stuyvesant sent seven vessels to conquer New Sweden in 1655, Falkinburg set up housekeeping on Burlington Island on the Delaware River. This was a piece of land on the east side of the Delaware River, in Burlington County. At the time, it was the farthest north on the Delaware River that any white man had settled. Falkinburg thus lived on the furthest outpost of civilization in those days.

The Swedes had surrendered to the Dutch without firing a shot, and now it was the Netherlanders' turn to capitulate when the English fleet sailed into Delaware Bay. When the English ship *Kent* arrived in 1677, the Quaker commissioner found Falkinburg and engaged him as interpreter in the purchase of land from the Indians. Whatever the case, Falkinburg seems to have enjoyed the confidences of the Dutch, Swedes, Indians, and English, and he was considered something of a linguist.

Falkinburg's work was rewarded on October 10, 1677, when the English purchased the land between Rancocas Creek and the Assanpink at Trenton from the Indians. Falkinburg was the interpreter, and the deed was signed by several chiefs, including Ockaniekon. Various items these Indians received in compensation included 30 blankets, 30 guns, 30 kettles, 30 looking glasses, 30 Jews'

5

harps, and 30 scissors. In those days, these items represented a considerable amount of wealth. In the New World, there were few manufactured or finished goods. A 1745 estate of a fairly wealthy New Englander mentioned the following: "four gold coins, one Bible, one saddle, one cow, one shoe-making set, one looking glass, one wash tub and two churns, one tin stove, two axes, two mares, two bed-stands, and one pewter teapot." Years later, the Indian chief and negotiator Wilted Grass would reflect on treaties like this and say in 1832: "Not a drop of our blood have you spilled in battle; not an acre of our land have you taken but by our consent."

When Sir Edmund Andros was placed in charge of the English colonies in the New World, Falkinburg was forced to leave the island and it was leased to Robert Stacy, who had connections in England. According to Burlington County historian George DeCou, "Many of the pioneers felt that it was unjust and unfair to dispossess Falkinburg and rent the island to Stacy, as Falkinburg had been a great service to them by acting as their interpreter with the Indians."

Forced to leave Burlington, Falkinburg hiked across the Pine Barrens and opened up the Little Egg Harbor area along the Atlantic seaboard. On February 7, 1698, he purchased 800 acres of land from the Lenape Indians. Included in these lands were Osborn Island, Wills Island, and parts of the mainland. His first dwelling place was a cave, which he dug; his occupations included hunter, fisherman, oysterman, and housekeeper. When his first wife died, he set out on foot to Swedesboro to find a wife. He was successful and returned to Little Egg Harbor where local Quakers and his Indian friends attended the marriage ceremony. Their first child was born in a cave. Later, the Falkinburgs built a large farmhouse on the land that became known as Elihu Mathis Farm. Following Falkinburg's lead, other settlers came and soon Little Egg Harbor was a thriving community.

Falkinburg's descendants included many sea captains, a state assemblyman from Cape May, and many others including Jennifer Mott Palermo, who researched much of this information. Of her ancestor, Palermo said: "Henry Jacobs Falkinburg exemplified the pioneer spirit of someone who was strong physically, mentally, and spiritually. He lived off the land and was able to survive in the wilderness. He was a good negotiator and was able to win friendship with the Indians and learn their language. He believed in treating the Indians right and his reputation followed him. Falkinburg was a great American and left a great legacy."

Johann Printz:
He Ruled with a Heavy Hand

Johann Printz ruled with the heaviest hand of any New Jersey governor. His hand *had* to be the heaviest: Altogether he weighed over 400 pounds. Historical records indicate that he wasn't afraid to throw that weight around; he was a virtual dictator.

Johann Printz was a controversial figure even before he came to America. He had been removed from his position as a lieutenant colonel in the Swedish Cavalry (pity the poor horse that had to carry him) in 1640 for failing to obtain a passport when he returned to Sweden from a German campaign. Anxious to redeem himself and quick to see the personal advantages, Printz accepted the post of Governor of New Sweden when the Dutch West India Company offered it to him in 1642.

The gangplank must have sagged and groaned beneath his weight as he carried his 7-foot frame off the Swedish ship at Fort Christiana in Delaware. Despite his enormous weight, he was a bundle of energy. First, he told the colonists what he intended to do. New Sweden would start producing wine, grow walnut trees and press oil from walnuts, pursue whaling and fishing—and an occasional Spanish galleon—extract salt from the waves, and expand the fur-trade with the Indians. His intention was to carve a commercial and military empire out of the Delaware Valley. Delaware Bay would be a Swedish lake, the New Jersey countryside a smorgasbord of bounty for thousands of Swedish colonists.

Then he told them how the Queen had charged him with converting the Indians to Lutheranism. According to his orders, he was to "understand how to treat them with all humanity and respect, that no violence or wrong be done them by Her Royal Majesty or her subjects." On this item he proved true to his word and the Queen's command. To this day, the Swedes are considered to have had the best record of any pioneer group in their treatment of the Indians.

In order to strengthen New Sweden's hold on the Delaware Valley, Printz set to work immediately building a fort on the east bank of the river. Named Fort Elfsborg after a Swedish fort near Gothenberg, it was built near what is now

Salem. Situated on a high bluff, the fort offered a commanding view in all directions. Ships wishing to sail past were required to strike their flags, put in, and pay tribute to the Swedish Crown. Legend has it that if the Swedes were forced to fire a cannonball to stop an offending ship, the captain had to pay for the cost of the cannonball along with the tribute. What ships would have been sailing up the Delaware? They were usually English and Dutch ships, the former to reinforce their colony at Vaarkens Kill (near Burlington), the latter to supply their colony at Ft. Nassau (near Philadelphia). With the opening of Ft. Elfsborg, Swedes became the dominant colonial power in the Delaware Valley.

Even before Elfsborg was complete, Printz set to work on another fort—Fort New Gothenburg—on an island off present-day Gibbstown in Gloucester County. Here Printz built a stately mansion, which was said to have been the finest between Virginia and New York. (It was the *only* mansion between Virginia and New York!) From his base on Tinicum Island, Printz often went sailing on the Delaware, making him the first American yachtsman.

Over the next few years, Printz settled down to rule his feudal barony. He rescued English Virginia governor Lord Plowden, who had been shipwrecked by a scheming skipper; prosecuted George Lamberton, an English settler who had sought to stir up the Indians against the Swedes; sent ship-loads of tobacco back to Sweden; and oversaw the building of several ships, an old Swedish industry. One thing that he lacked was a secretary to help him perform his work. In a letter to the New Sweden Company, Printz asked that a Latin secretary (not a Spanish beauty, but a scholar who would write in Latin) be sent to him, "especially since I have more often for the last 27 years had the musket and the pistol in my hands than Tacitus or Cicero. . ."

Unfortunately, not even Printz could hold New Sweden together for his country. Supplies, reinforcements, and settlers never came in large numbers, sealing the colony's fate. Discouraged, Printz returned to Sweden in 1654. Two years later, Dutch forces under Governor Stuyvesant conquered Swedish settlements without firing a shot.

Today, Governor Printz looms "large" in New Jersey history. He was the heaviest man to ever serve as a New Jersey governor. In today's health-conscious society, in which New Jersey governors eat quiche and drink mineral water, the odds are he'll keep that distinction.

Photo is courtesy of The New Jersey Historical Society.

JOHN FENWICK: FOUNDER OF SALEM

When John Fenwick sailed up a small New Jersey river on November 23, 1675, he was so struck by the tranquility of the South Jersey countryside that he named it after the Hebrew word for peace.

"Its name shall be Salem," said Fenwick. Thus was born the town and the county of Salem. Unfortunately, Fenwick himself never knew of true peace; trouble dogged him all his life, both in England and in America.

Fenwick first gained a stake in America when he agreed to serve as an agent for a fellow Quaker, Edward Byllynge, and purchased half of New Jersey for the price of 1,000 pounds. (Byllynge was in financial trouble at the time, and couldn't consummate the deal without incurring the wrath of his creditors.) Byllynge's affairs eventually became so involved that three Quaker trustees—including young William Penn—were appointed to oversee his estate until he could get his finances in order.

Plans were made for a colony, complete with republican government and freedom of religion—features that would set important precedents for the future United States. But Fenwick was never paid back for his original 1,000-pound investment, or so Fenwick claimed. Instead, he was given 10 of the 100 shares of New Jersey land available.

Fenwick took his case to court, where Penn was appointed arbiter. Penn decided in favor of Byllynge and his creditors, and Fenwick, who thought he owned half of New Jersey, was left only with Salem and Cumberland counties.

Fenwick complained bitterly to Penn, but Penn urged him to put aside his ill feelings and get on with life and business.

"Away with vain fancies, I entreat thee," Penn advised. "Follow closely to thy business, thy days spend on, and make the best of what thou hast. Thy grandchildren may be in the other world before what thou has allotted will be employed." In other words, "Don't cry over spilt milk; you won't even be able to take care of what you have." It was good advice, and, at least outwardly, Fenwick seemed undeterred in his goal of founding a colony in New Jersey, called

West Jersey in those days. Fenwick plowed ahead of the other shareholders and organized his own expedition to the wilds of South Jersey.

To this day, no one knows for sure who really should have had title to that land. Did Byllynge put up the original 1,000 pounds or was it really Fenwick's money? The whole incident gives credence to what both Fenwick and Penn must have read in their Bibles: "My son, if thou be surety for thy neighbor, thou art snared with the words of thy mouth" (Proverbs 6:1).

When Fenwick set sail from the south coast of England in the summer of 1675, on board were his two married daughters, Mrs. John Addams and Mrs. Edward Chamneys, their husbands and children, a son John, and an unmarried daughter, Anna. It was a real family affair, although Mrs. Fenwick was left behind to be sent for after the colony was founded. In addition to Fenwick's family, there was somewhere between 50 and 200 other people on board their ship, the *Griffin*.

Although Fenwick had been given clear title to his share of the land, he, nevertheless, wanted to be sure and consolidated his claim by buying the land from the Indians, as had Peter Minuit, and it was bought for $24 in goods.

According to tradition, the deal between Fenwick and the Indians was sealed under the Salem Oak, which still stands, spreading its majestic boughs over Quaker Cemetery. Fenwick's Indians drove a harder bargain than had Minuit's: In exchange for the land, Fenwick gave the Indians guns, powder, and 300 gallons of rum. Years later, a white man could be hanged for selling guns and liquor to the Indians; fortunately, the Lenape were generally very peaceful Indians.

Having strengthened his claim to what became known as Fenwick's Tenth, Fenwick set to work building the colony. "If there's any terrestrial Canaan," wrote Fenwick, "tis surely here, where land floweth with milk and honey." Fenwick also planned villages at Cohanzick (Greenwich of tea-burning fame) and Finn's Point, but didn't live long enough to see them come into existence.

In order to finance his estate building, Fenwick mortgaged his property to John Eldridge and Edmund Warner. Eldridge and Warner considered this a transfer of all rights to them. William Penn and the other trustees, still upset that Fenwick had rushed ahead of them with his colonizing plans, sided with Eldridge and Warner, as did the county. On August 18, 1676, the trustees appointed commissioners to tell Fenwick that he could only sell land with the approval of the trustees. If Fenwick would cooperate with them, the trustees said, his 10 shares would be on an equal basis with theirs.

But this wasn't the end of Fenwick's troubles. Not only did he lose his property, he also lost his freedom. When the king of England sent Sir Edmund Andros to America to consolidate the colonies, Andros claimed Salem. A defiant Fenwick was jailed, only to be released when the Andros experiment began to fail. Resistance against royal tyranny by New Jerseyans like Fenwick helped to establish a precedent for freedom that would eventually lead to the creation of the American Republic in 1787.

In 1682, Fenwick and Penn were reconciled, and Fenwick turned most of his rights over to Penn and his "Holy Experiment." Old and full of days, Fenwick died in 1683. Thus, the man who would have made an empire out of southern New Jersey wound up with just 6 feet of earth.

Despite his trials, Fenwick is remembered today for his role in getting William Penn interested in America, in founding Salem, and for his courage against overwhelming odds.

Berkeley and Carteret:
They Once Owned New Jersey

Most people are familiar with the real estate empires of Charles Landis (Vineland, 19th century) and Donald Trump (Atlantic City, 20th century). But these men's holdings pale into insignificance when compared with that of Lord John Berkeley and Sir George Carteret. For in the late 1600s, these men owned the whole of New Jersey, from Cape May to the Highlands, from the Delaware to the Palisades.

What is now New Jersey was part of the huge territories that English King Charles II granted in 1664 to his brother James, the Duke of York. A day later, James granted New Jersey to Berkeley and Carteret, concentrating his efforts on New York and building the English Navy. For Berkeley and Carteret, James was a friend indeed.

Albania, as New Jersey was briefly called, then contained small bands of Dutch and Swedish settlers. It remained for Carteret and Berkeley to promote these holdings in England. The first thing they did was to name the colony after the place of Carteret's birth, and where he had also served as governor, the Isle of Jersey. Jersey was also known as Caesarea (*Jer* is a contraction of Caesar and *ey* signifies island. It was thought that Julius Caesar stopped there on his way to invade England). In New Jersey's early history, it was sometimes called Nova Caesarea. Today, the isle of Jersey is known as a tax haven, a banking center, the source of the Jersey cow, and of potatoes the size of grapes.

Early correspondence indicated that New Jersey was the best of the Duke of York's grant, since it was reported to have fertile soil, excellent rivers, and a fine seacoast. To further induce English settlers to come, heads of families arriving by 1666 were granted 150 acres plus 150 more for each servant. Once a servant's term of service had expired, he had to be given 75 acres of land. Ministers of the Gospel were given 200 free acres of land to encourage the religious development of the colony. In all, not bad prices—try buying 75 acres of New Jersey land today! There were just three problems: The land was undeveloped, there was little market for whatever was produced there, and you took your life into your hands each time you took the dangerous journey to America.

13

Soon New Jersey was divided into two basic colonies, East Jersey, or North Jersey, and West Jersey, or South Jersey. In the early days, South Jersey was often referred to as Down Jersey. With this being settled, Carteret and Berkeley began a massive real estate sale. Most of South Jersey was sold in Tenths for others to develop. A group of Irishmen bought the Irish Tenth in present-day Gloucester County, while John Fenwick, a Quaker, bought the Fenwick Tenth in what is now Salem.

Who were these men, our earliest real estate developers? Sir George Carteret had been a naval officer who had joined the Navy as a boy and worked his way up through the ranks (unusual in those days of the aristocracy's domination of the officer class). In 1639 he became a comptroller of the English Navy. During the English Civil War he governed the island of Jersey and fought for the king but lost. When the king was restored to power in 1660, because of his undying loyalty, Carteret was rewarded with the office of Treasurer of the Navy, and later, with New Jersey.

Lord John Berkeley was another friend of the king, although not as highly esteemed as Carteret. In fact, some contemporaries described him as "vain, selfish, lacking in tact, and a place-seeker." But he was willing to suffer with the young king when he was exiled from his country to France. Thus, when King Charles was restored to power (England had briefly tried a commonwealth form of government), Berkeley was rewarded for his services. Among his rewards: the position of Lord Lieutenant of Ireland and proprietor of the colony of New Jersey.

In 1674, Berkeley sold his interest in New Jersey to John Fenwick, while Carteret died in 1680. At Carteret's death, the New Jersey colony was run first by his estate (24 proprietors) and later by a number of unsatisfactory governments, including the governor of New York, who claimed that New York owned New Jersey! In 1701, after a virtual rebellion of many people who wanted a better government, New Jersey became a royal colony, ruled directly by the king and his handpicked governor. (In those days, governors were appointed by the king). So it was that two men—Lord John Berkeley and Sir George Carteret—owned New Jersey for a brief time. They must have put New Jersey on a sound footing, since today it is the most densely populated state in the nation. The moral of the story? I suppose it's "be true to your friends," especially if one of those friends is a king.

CAPTAIN KIDD: THIS PIRATE ONCE SAILED SOUTH JERSEY'S WATERS

In the late 1600s a boy was born in Greenock, Scotland. Surrounded by the rigorous moral teachings of the Church of Scotland and the hardy Scottish Covenantors (some of whom later settled in the Batsto area), he chose to reject his background and entered a life of crime. He became Captain William Kidd, the notorious pirate. Much of his professional life would be spent sailing in and around South Jersey, which for a time in its early history was a haven for pirates.

In old South Jersey, the mouth of the Delaware was a general rendezvous for merchantmen with their riches from the East and West Indies, making this area prime hunting ground for pirates. The merchantmen's cargoes were destined for New York, New England, and Burlington (then West Jersey's capital), but often found their way into a pirate's treasure trove. This area was made even more conducive to pirates due to Philadelphia's lack of naval and military strength and the reluctance of the peace-loving Quakers to hang such rascals. Delaware Bay and the barrier islands off Atlantic and Cape May counties became something of a resort for these outlaw vessels and were used for repair of their ships.

That Captain Kidd was active in South Jersey waters there can be no doubt. Colonel Robert Quarry, Judge of the Admiralty, reported to the Lords of Trade on June 1, 1699, that "there had arrived sixty pirates in a ship directly from Madagascar. They are part of Kidd's gang. About sixteen of them have quitted the ship and are landed in ye government of West Jersey at Cape May. The rest of them are still on board the ship which lies at anchor near ye Cape of this government waiting for sloops from New York to unload here. . . I seized two of these pirates and conveyed them safely to the Burlington jail."

In a subsequent report, Colonel Quarry tells of the assistance of Governor Bass of the Jerseys, and how more pirates at Cape May were apprehended. Treasure recovered from these pirates included "rix-dollar (a small Dutch coin), Arabian and Christian gold, amber and cord necklaces, India silks and other costly goods of the Indies." On one occasion, Gov. Bass records that he saw Captain

Kidd's sloop himself—a large ship with 60 hands. Unfortunately, Kidd's vessel outsailed the government ship and escaped.

According to local legend, in 1699 the barkentine which served as Kidd's flagship was once anchored near the mouth of Brigantine Inlet, just north of what is now Atlantic City. Captain Kidd, his mate Timothy Jones, and several of the crew came ashore and buried a sea chest in the sand dunes. Later, according to the legend, Kidd and Jones returned, dug up the chest, and re-buried it elsewhere. A fight between Jones and Kidd resulted in Jones' death. The loot has never been found.

Other sites where buried pirates' treasures are reported to have been buried include Five Mile Beach, Marcus Hook (Pennsylvania), and Cape May Point. At Cape May Point, a large cedar tree once stood near where a treasure was supposed to have been buried. It was called the Captain Kidd Treasure Tree.

Some South Jersey settlers were ambivalent about pirates like Kidd, since they often spent lavishly in the cash-poor settlements along the Jersey coast. But pirates didn't live the glorified lives we sometimes see on television or read about in adventure novels. In fact, their lives were short, nasty, and brutish. They were violent, promiscuous, and subject to frequent diseases. It didn't take long for their presence to become intolerable among the increasing numbers of settled families that called South Jersey home. As local government's resources increased, and the British Navy began to weigh down on piracy, this form of terrorism came to an end.

Captain Kidd, who was originally a privateer in the service of the English government, eventually went over to the other side. At first he captured enemy ships as he was instructed, but soon he was attacking the ships of countries friendly to England. The English government declared him a pirate. He was arrested in Boston and sent to England for trial. Kidd's defense was that he had been forced to commit acts of piracy by his mutinous crew, but the jury found him guilty and he was hanged.

Does any of Kidd's treasure still exist today? The legends say yes, so keep your eyes open at the beach and your metal detector handy. My guess, however, is that you'd be better off investing monthly in a good mutual fund or legacy stock.

CASPAR WISTAR:
FATHER OF THE AMERICAN GLASS INDUSTRY

What steel was to Pittsburgh and coal to Newcastle (England), glassmaking was to New Jersey. Years ago, South Jersey was the leading glassmaking center in the nation. Place names like "Glassboro" serve as a reminder of that heritage, while the details of the story are filled in at museums like Wheaton Village in Millville.

So important was glass to New Jersey that towns like Millville and Clayton were built on glass. When glassmaking was at its height, Jersey glass was advertised and sold all over the world. One could find Jersey glass even on the tables of royalty in Europe.

The story of Jersey glass begins with Caspar Wistar, who might well be dubbed "The Father of American Glass." Wistar's contribution to founding the glass industry is so significant that his life is the story of Jersey glass in its early years.

Wistar was born in 1696 in the little German city of Heidelberg. Like many Germans, Wistar was impressed by the claims made by William Penn's German representatives, who promised a better life in the New World. And so in the early summer of 1717, Wistar packed his few belongings and got on a ship bound for Philadelphia.

Unlike most Germans who arrived in Philadelphia in the 1700s who settled in Germantown or west towards Lancaster, Wistar crossed the Delaware River and settled in Salem County. Seeing that southern New Jersey had the main ingredients for glassmaking, Wistar set up the first permanent glassmaking operation in the New World. Ironically, Wistar knew very little about glassmaking—he was a buttonmaker. But Wistar was first and foremost a businessman, and he saw that his future was in glass, not buttons.

Twenty-one years after arriving in America, Wistar sent to Germany for four experts who could come to America and teach the art of glassmaking to him and his son. On December 7, 1738, responding to Wistar's call and promise of profits, Caspar Halter, John Halter, Johannis Wentzel, and Simeon Kreismayer left the port of Rotterdam for America. When the Palatinate Germans arrived, they found that their partner had acquired about 2,000 acres of land on Alloways

Creek near the city of Salem. The land was rich in white sand and trees that could be used as fuel.

The first Wistar furnace was put into operation during the fall of 1739. Soon a small village grew up around the glassworks, which became known as Wistarburg. The factory worked full blast from the start, turning out window glass, wine and spirits bottles, snuff canisters, and mustard jars. It also produced glass for the electrical experiments of Wistar's Philadelphia neighbor, Benjamin Franklin. Soon the factory was filling orders for other scientists as far away as New York, New Haven, and Jamaica.

The Wistarburg glass that would be most prized later on were small, useful or decorative pieces turned out by the workers in their free time with the material left in the pots at the end of the day. These pieces included bowls, pitchers, candlestick holders, rolling pins or vases of pale aquamarine window glass or of amber, olive, or dark green glass used for jars and bottles.

Caspar's son Richard continued the glass factory until he died in 1781. After his death, no one else had the entrepreneurial skills to combine laborers, South Jersey's resources, and markets together as the Wistars had done. Today, experts estimate that there are less than 30 original pieces of Wistar glass left in the world. Much of the rest has been broken into pieces so small that they've gone back to their original state—sand.

Oh, and there's one more thing: Caspar Wistar, "The Father of American Glass," never learned how to blow or make glass himself. His talent was in bringing everything needed to make glass together, and then selling it. Such business skills are, in the end, sometimes more rare than a skill like glassblowing. Yet they are absolutely essential, as they create new enterprises, new jobs, and sometimes beautiful works of art, like Wistarburg glass.

Daniel Leeds:
Author of America's First Almanac

In colonial days, next to the Bible, the most important book was the almanac. No matter how far out on the frontier a family was, one could almost always find an almanac next to the musket hanging on the wall. And, like so many other things, one of the first American almanacs was written in New Jersey by Daniel Leeds.

Ben Franklin was perhaps the greatest promoter of the almanac in colonial America. Certainly his *Poor Richard's Almanac* sold thousands of copies and helped give him the independent wealth he needed to pursue his political interests. But it was our own Daniel Leeds who gave Franklin the idea.

Daniel Leeds was one of Galloway Township's (and Burlington County's) first settlers. Leeds was born in Leeds, England, in 1652 and came to America in 1678. First settling near Jackson, he began to expand his real estate holdings throughout the state. Eventually, he held most of the land between Smithville to Motts Creek to Lower Island. While living at what he called Leeds Point, he became the first Surveyor General of West Jersey.

Like so many other early South Jerseyans, Daniel Leeds was a Quaker—that is, until after the death of his second wife, when he became an Episcopalian.

In 1687, Leeds published his first almanac, having the printing done by the Bradford family in Philadelphia. Leeds often complained of the difficult trip from Leeds Point to Philadelphia to get his manuscripts published. Yet it was apparently worth the effort. He continued to write his almanac until 1716, after which three of his sons—Felix, Titan, and Philo—carried on the work.

Just what exactly did almanacs like Leeds' contain? Most of us are familiar with Franklin's almanac, which contained such sage advice as this: "Then plow deep while sluggards sleep, and you shall have corn to sell, and to keep." But giving sage advice wasn't the main purpose of the almanac. The almanac was, above all else, about the weather. And rightly so, for, to our American and New Jersey forefathers, the weather was all-important. Over 90 percent of the people were farmers. Thus, the hours of the rising and setting of the sun, the cycle of the moon and the tide, and the prospects of weather were the timetables of the average man's life, as necessary to him as the subway or airplane schedule is to the modern commuter. The almanac told of the date of court sessions and the schedule of post riders, coaches, and packet boats. It combined all the features of *Better Homes and Gardens, Popular Mechanics,* and the *Reader's Digest.* It was indispensable to colonial life. Accordingly, old issues were preserved and used to pass the time on long winter nights or to amuse some overnight guest. Almanacs even helped to spread up-to-date political information here and throughout the colonies just before the Revolution.

Today, both the Leeds name and the almanac live on in American history. Daniel Leeds left many descendants—so many, in fact, that for a time it seemed that one could hardly throw a stone in a South Jersey schoolyard without hitting a Leeds. Daniel Leeds himself became unpopular because of his support of Edward Hyde, the dictatorial governor of New Jersey, but his name lives on in Leeds Point, several Leeds Avenues, and old Mother Leeds, who supposedly gave birth to the Jersey Devil. (The Jersey Devil was apparently a Leeds, at least on his mother's side!)

As for the almanac that Leeds helped to pioneer, distant descendants are still published under the names of the *Farmer's Almanac* and *Old Farmer's Almanac.* These books still contain lots of useful information. This year, why not pick one up and enjoy its wit, wisdom, and weather—a tradition started by New Jersey's own Daniel Leeds.

Blackbeard the Pirate: Terror of the Barrier Islands

Legend has it that Blackbeard the Pirate had a hideout on the Mullica River and frequently visited the Delaware Bay and River. If the story is true, he probably isn't the first pirate, nor will he be the last, to call New Jersey his home.

Throughout the Colonial Era, the Jersey coast was often visited by pirates, who took advantage of the many rivers, coves, and other hiding places afforded by the barrier islands. During the Revolution, the line between pirates and patriots was thin indeed. The privateers who preyed on British ships were called Patriots by the Americans but pirates by our English brethren across the sea. This no doubt confirmed—at least in British eyes—the opinion of Samuel Johnson, who said that "patriotism is the last refuge of a scoundrel" and that "every American rebel ought to be hanged immediately from the nearest tree." Yes, patriots and scoundrels frequented Jersey waters, but the worst scoundrel of them all had to be Blackbeard the Pirate.

Born Edward Teach, either in Bristol, England, or in Jamaica (no one knows for sure), Blackbeard received his name from the habit of braiding his long, black beard and tying the braids with ribbon. He is considered to be the fiercest pirate who ever lived, making himself look even more devilish by wearing a fur cap with two slowburning cannon fuses (made of hemp cord dipped in saltpeter and limewater), which had the effect of enveloping his head in a halo of black smoke.

Not content with waiting for the afterlife to receive the due reward of his deeds, Blackbeard made a hell of life on Earth for all around him. When things were slow, Blackbeard would say, "Come, let us make a hell of our own and try how long we can bear it." Accordingly, he (with two or three others) went down into the hold of his ship and, closing up all the hatches, filled several pots full of brimstone and set them on fire. Whoever didn't suffocate or cry out for air was the winner. Blackbeard always held out the longest.

Blackbeard had more than twice as many wives as Henry VIII. Over the years, a total of 13 young women boarded Blackbeard's ship to stand up next to him before the first mate, who solemnly pronounced them man and wife. But be-

21

"Who'll guard this wealth?" bold Blackbeard cried. . . .

Artwork by Richard C. Moore is courtesy of The Burlington County Cultural and Heritage Commission.

fore the ink was dry on the marriage license, Blackbeard would sail away looking for a girl in another port.

In the early years of his career, Blackbeard is said to have frequented a tavern at Second and High Streets in Philadelphia. Across the Delaware River, in Burlington County, Blackbeard purchased the flour and ham necessary for his trips. It is also thought that he may have buried a treasure in Burlington at the foot of Wood Street.

But Burlington wasn't the only place in South Jersey that Teach supposedly visited. According to legend, Blackbeard had a hideout on an island in the Mullica River. He may even have divided treasure up on High Bank, several miles up on the river from the bay.

Blackbeard took such a toll on shipping and created so much terror along the Atlantic seaboard that plantation owners in Virginia and the Carolinas organized against him. The Virginia governor sent the ship *H.M.S. Pearl* out to take him dead or alive. He was caught on November 21, 1718, near Ocracoke Inlet, off the North Carolina coast. Even though he fought desperately, he finally fell from the more than 25 wounds that had been inflicted upon him. His head was cut off, taken back to Virginia, and impaled on a pole, black beard and all.

How much of this story is true? There was indeed an Edward Teach, known as Blackbeard, and he did frequent the Jersey coast. We also know that he was killed by authorities from Virginia. The rest is difficult to verify. One thing is for sure—Blackbeard wouldn't be the last "scum" to show up on New Jersey's shores.

Elizabeth Haddon:
She Founded Haddonfield for Love

As far as we know, Haddonfield, New Jersey, is the only colonial town founded specifically by a woman. Other towns were founded by men, or by men and women as part of families, but Haddonfield was founded by a determined Quaker miss, Elizabeth Haddon, who followed her heart. But even more intriguing is the tale of her romance with John Estaugh, later immortalized by Henry Wadsworth Longfellow.

Born in London to a prosperous Quaker family, Elizabeth met John, a young Quaker missionary, in 1695. Although she was only 14, their conversations were enough to convince her that this was the man the Lord had intended for her.

But it was love for another man, her father, which induced her to go to America. John Haddon had purchased a 500-acre plantation in West Jersey (now South Jersey) in 1698. By 1701, Haddon had developed such confidence in his 20-year-old daughter that he sent her to America to develop the property. For Elizabeth, the pot was sweetened by the fact that John Estaugh had left a few months earlier to preach in the southern colonies. True, there were wide expanses in the wilds of America, but the fact that there were so few settlements helped to make it a "small world." Thus, there was a good chance the two would see each other again.

Elizabeth Haddon reached Philadelphia in the spring of 1701 and impressed those who met her with her good education, deep religious convictions, and good judgment. Eventually, she crossed the Delaware and traveled up the Cooper River about 10 miles, where she took up residence in a log cabin.

Longfellow, in "The Theologian's Tale" pictures her as leading a rather gracious life, sending servants off to the village with "hampers of food and clothing" for the poor. Her home became a way station for traveling Quakers—"they come and they tarry, as if thy house were a tavern," Longfellow has her housemaid say in the poem.

Then one fine day John Estaugh came north from Virginia, and the two met again. Tradition says that Elizabeth did the speaking as the pair rode to Sunday Meeting. Longfellow imagines her as saying: "I will no longer conceal what is laid upon me to tell thee, I have received from the Lord a charge to love thee, John Estaugh." Shocked yet pleased by this boldness, Estaugh supposedly muttered how impressed he was with her, but concluded: "I have yet no light to lead me, no voice to direct me." Elizabeth told him that she would wait while he waited for "guidance." Elizabeth wondered, as Longfellow put it, if they would be but "ships that pass in the night." But she needn't have worried. Estaugh soon saw the light, and was back within a few months to marry her.

The Estaughs moved into a new two-story brick house in 1713, built on the site of modern Haddonfield. Round them the town grew, taking its name from Elizabeth. By the time of the Revolution, Haddonfield had become important enough to be the scene of major activity as both British and Patriot forces passed through the town. The historic Creighton House, or Indian King Tavern, served as headquarters for the Provincial Assembly when Hessian troops occupied Trenton. After the war, the state assembly met there for a while. Today, Haddonfield is a beautiful, historic town with many interesting and well-stocked shops and family businesses, a town that still shows the influence of "a woman's touch." And that woman was Elizabeth Haddon.

KING NUMMY:
SOUTH JERSEY'S ONE AND ONLY KING

Most Americans find it fascinating to read about the latest exploits—and antics—of Britain's royal family. Three hundred years ago, we had our own royalty. His name was King Nummy, the Indian chief whose name has been stamped indelibly on local maps and legends.

According to most local historians, King Nummy (or Nammis or Natimus) was the last Indian chief to live in South Jersey. One story says he tried to lead the Lenape out of South Jersey to escape white settlers' influence, while another says that Nummy remained behind to die and be buried in his ancestral homeland.

King Nummy was a leader of the Kechameches, a band of Lenape Indians who were South Jersey's first shore visitors. During the winter, they would retreat to their wigwams near present-day Vineland and Bridgeton, while in the summer they would camp along the shore to go fishing, clamming, and crabbing.

The Lenapes had no written language, metals, wheels, guns, or farm animals. But they did have an important role among their fellow Algonquin-speaking tribes. Soon after settling in New Jersey, they had accepted the job of being a buffer between warring tribes, becoming a "peace tribe." South Jersey's peaceful Indians helped to set the pattern for the typical South Jerseyan: peace loving, easy-going, "laid-back," and non-confrontational. King Nummy represented this tradition well, giving the original "Cape May Diamond" to Christopher Leaming as a token of friendship.

The Lenapes were divided into three clans: the Wolf, Turkey, and Turtle. When not dining on fish or dried seafood, the Lenape also ate corn pudding, bread, beans, squash, fruit, wild game, and venison. In March, some Indians would go to the Delaware to catch shad. As the Lenape moved back and forth across South Jersey, their trails formed the basis of South Jersey's first roads. Their practice was to go around all obstacles, usually making their trails rather crooked. This is one reason why a number of South Jersey roads today are crooked even though they do not have to be. The Lenape believed in life after death, burying their dead in a coffin, and showering its occupant with gifts to use in the next life.

The Lenape, like most Indians, were communal in their approach to property. The men concentrated on hunting, while the women worked small gardens. As would befit a king, Nummy had an interest in other economic pursuits. In one of the few references to him in Cape May County documents, there is a record of him selling a whale to settler Evan Davis (whaling was once a big Cape May industry).

The Lenapes were the first to recognize the value of the cranberry, using it as a symbol of peace. At gatherings, a bowl of cranberries would be passed around as other tribes would pass around a peace pipe.

But in the late 1600s, life was no bowl of cranberries for the remaining Lenape (their numbers were never more than a few thousand). Legend says that they met in council and decided the Great Spirit was angry with them so they packed up and left the area. The next 150 years saw them move from central Jersey to New York to Green Bay, Wisconsin.

Nummy probably stayed, as some tell it, to care for the child of his sister Snowflower and to die in the sandy forests of South Jersey. Some say he's buried at Nummytown, at the head of Fishing Creek in Cape May, or on Nummy Island, along Ocean Drive between North Wildwood and Stone Harbor. In addition to these two locations, he also gave his name to Nummy Trail, Nummy Lake in Belleplain State Forest, and Nummy Campground in Middle Township.

Whatever the truth is about South Jersey's only king, this is for sure: When King Nummy disappeared off the stage of South Jersey history, one era had come to an end and a new one had begun.

Photo of Lenape Indian in front of Mays Landing Courthouse is by Thomas H. Hogan, IV.

ELIZABETH BODLY:
SHE FOUNDED A THRIVING PORT

Today, Port Elizabeth is a sleepy little town along the Maurice River just south of Millville in Cumberland County. But like so many other places in South Jersey, it has a great history. In fact, it was once a leading city in the world of our colonial forebears. And what's more, it was founded by a woman, Elizabeth Ray Bodly. Now just a tiny landing on the Maurice River (named by Dutch explorers for Prince Maurice of Holland), Port Elizabeth was once a port of call for ships coming directly from the West Indies, loaded with rum, molasses, and other exotic products.

Some say that Elizabeth Bodly was descended from Swedish royalty, but that's probably not true. Most of the Swedes and Finns that came over were poor people with little or no prospects in the Old World. Whatever the case, she was the daughter of John Ray and was born in what is now Pilesgrove Township, Salem County, in 1737.

At a fairly young age, (the average life span in those days was 35 years), Elizabeth married Cornelius Clark, a native of Burlington. Together, they bought a large tract of land near the Maurice River. Calling a log house their home (the log cabin was one of Sweden's gifts to the New World), they had four children: Joel, John, Susan, and Elizabeth. But Cornelius died young—as did so many other people in the harsh environment of colonial South Jersey. Elizabeth was left to fend for herself, her farm, and her children, yet she was regarded as having the best meadowland for harvest in the area.

Whether it was her determination, her beauty, or even her meadowland, she attracted the attention of John Bodly, a nearby pioneer. The two united, and she had two more children. Shortly thereafter, Elizabeth's second husband died. It was about this time that the town became known as Port Elizabeth in honor of this steadfast woman. Her farm was prosperous enough to allow her to become a local philanthropist, and those in need would often beat a path to her door. A Quaker, she was duty-bound to help the less fortunate.

As one would expect of a town builder, Elizabeth employed surveyors to plot the village, bounded on the north by Broadway, on the east by Second Street, on the south by Quaker Street, and on the west by Front Street. In 1789, Port Elizabeth was made an official port of delivery, while a post office was established in 1802, making it a local communications center. Businesses founded in Bodly's day included the Union Glass Works, the Eagle Glass Works, and a hotel. Elizabeth Bodly also helped turn her town into a regionally known educational center, by deeding part of her land to the Federal School, a private school association. Also founded was the Port Elizabeth Academy, another prominent private school. These private schools were actually public schools, since they were open to the public for a small fee and there were no public schools as we know them today.

Elizabeth Bodly died on November 25, 1815, at the age of 78. Her name still clings to the village she founded, but much of the former glory is gone. Millville eventually supplanted Port Elizabeth in importance and in glassmaking. Also, nearby towns such as Bivalve and Port Norris became major centers of the oyster industry. The oyster industry has since died out, much of the seedbeds having been wiped out by disease in the 1950s and 60s. (Scientists are now making efforts to re-seed the beds and revitalize the South Jersey oyster industry, albeit on a modest level.)

John Brainerd: Founder of America's First Indian Reservation

In the 1700s South Jersey was still a frontier, and people were few and far between. The last of the Lenape Indians still roamed through the Pine Barrens. These were the days of the circuit-riding preachers.

Circuit-riding preachers were needed, for no community had enough people to support an established church. Ministers and missionaries were forced to ride a "circuit," visiting Pleasant Mills near Batsto one Sunday—baptizing and marrying as many people as possible—preaching in Port Republic on Wednesday, and in Somers Point the following Sunday.

The most famous of these preachers in the 17th century was John Brainerd. Among other things, he helped to found the forerunner of the Pleasant Mills Church and set up the first Indian reservation in United States history, in what is now Burlington County.

Born in Britain, Brainerd came to America with high hopes. His brother, David, was a missionary whose expulsion from Yale for religious reasons led to the founding of Princeton University. Together they fanned out to minister to the people of New Jersey: David to the north, and John to the south.

David's life was cut short—he died at the age of 29 from tuberculosis—but his journal stands as a classic of American history and devotional literature. John, however, was blessed with good health, and worked for many years in South Jersey.

When John Brainerd arrived in South Jersey, he was pleasantly surprised to find a log church, erected by Scottish Covenanters at Neschochague. But the congregation soon outgrew this church, and Brainerd helped Captain Elijah Clark build a second church at The Forks in 1762. In Brainerd's journal, on April 25 of that year, he commented that he "officiated for the first time at the new meeting house at The Forks, erected since last fall, built of cedar logs, 25 feet square and ceiled with cedar." This was the Clark Meeting Church. The present Pleasant Mills–Batsto Chapel is the third church, built in 1808 on ground donated by Jesse Richards. It was dedicated by Methodist Bishop Francis Asbury in 1809 and named the Brainerd Church in memory of John. One of the first trustees was

Laurence Peterson, one of my ancestors. Brainerd's granddaughter, Sophia Ross, married Elijah Clark's son.

Brainerd felt called upon to carry the Gospel to the "destitute whites in need in the Pines" as well as to the Indians. His letter shows that he had to "supply (preach) at more than a half dozen places on the Lord's Day and preach lectures on other days at near twenty places, so large is this desolate country." Eventually there were a number of preaching stations called "Brainerd's churches." There was one at Bargaintown, where Zion Methodist Church now stands, and also one at Long-a-Coming (now Berlin).

Some of Brainerd's activities in the Batsto area included attending to the sick with prayer and psalm-reading and spending an evening settling a disagreement between a man and his wife, "bringing them to accord with God's help." One day, en route to Wading River, he lectured to people working at a cedar swamp and "spent time bodily laboring with the company clearing land, but taking care that they had not too much strong drink."

Eventually, small pockets of civilization began to emerge from the Pine Barrens. In 1775 Brainerd advised Reverend Philip Fithian (who led the Greenwich Tea Party) that the people at Elijah Clark's Meeting House "were nice in taste concerning preaching, expecting good speaking, good sense and sound divinity and from ministers with neatness and cleanliness in dress."

John's ministry in the Pines was supported by the Society of Scotland for Propagating Christian Knowledge. Between his Sunday preaching schedule, he made his home with the Indians. He both ministered to their needs and defended their rights. His diary recorded some of his work with the Indians: "Rode down country to settle an Indian affair and then to Bridgetown [now Mt. Holly] to consult respecting Indian lands at Wepinck and the cutting of timber by white men."

This concern for the Lenape led to the first Indian reservation in U.S. history, in Burlington County. Brainerd induced the colonial government to purchase 3,044 acres from Benjamin Springer for use by the Lenape (there were only about 500 left in 1760). The Indians called it Edgepillock; Brainerd called it Brotherton; today, it is called Indian Mills.

Brainerd envisioned a working, self-supporting community, and soon a settlement of several houses, a church, a school, a gristmill, and a sawmill were built. Unfortunately, Indian Mills only lasted for a few decades. Brainerd died just before the War of Independence. Most of the Lenapes left for upper New York state in 1802.

The life of John Brainerd—missionary to the Pines—is just one more chapter in the history of one of America's most historic regions, little South Jersey.

John Woolman:
Founder of the Anti-Slavery Movement

Long before the abolition movement and the Civil War, Down Jerseymen were fighting against slavery. Indeed, it might even be said that one New Jersey man— John Woolman of Mt. Holly—was the father of the efforts to end slavery in the United States. His nonviolent methods resulted in hundreds of masters agreeing to free their slaves, and in laws severely restricting or banning the slave trade. Because of Woolman, South Jersey became a center of anti-slavery activity, including the Underground Railway. Woolman's extreme humility, reflected in his life and writings, prevented him from making clear the importance of the part he played in the movement against slave holding. His compelling story deserves to be better known.

Born in 1720, on his family's Rancocas Farm in Burlington, he was raised in the Quaker tradition. He was given some training as a tailor, but was home-schooled and self-taught in book learning. From his earliest days, he showed evidence of a tender conscience and a serious mind. When just a teenager, he was upset with the way many people celebrated Christmas—resorting to public houses, and spending their time in drinking and vain sport, as he recorded in his journal.

But his righteous indignation was really roused while working as a clerk in a Mt. Holly store. His employer asked him to complete the sale of a slave woman, which he did against his conscience. He promised himself that from that time forward, he would take up the cause against slavery. And so this humble, peaceful Quaker began to fight slavery with a vengeance, the record of which we have in his tract, *Some Considerations on the Keeping of Negroes* (1754) and his *Journal* (1774). He correctly predicted that if slavery were not dealt with, a great tragedy would fall upon America.

On his first journey to the southern colonies he wrote: "I saw in these southern provinces so many vices and corruptions, increased by this trade and this way of life, that it appeared to me as a dark gloominess hanging over the land." Returning to New Jersey, he got his local Monthly Meeting's blessing for him to

32

Artwork is courtesy of the Burlington County Library, New Jersey Room, Mount Holly.

go out and preach against slavery. First, he traveled about South Jersey, going to small settlements in Salem, Cape May, Great and Little Egg Harbor, Manesquan, Manahawkin, and Barnegat. Then he went, either on foot or on horseback, to Pennsylvania, Delaware, Maryland, and Virginia.

To those who had no slaves, he preached: "In tender and most affectionate love I beseech you to keep clear from purchasing any." He told them that if they worked hard and lived with frugality, they would have no need of slaves. "Look to Divine Providence, and follow in simplicity that exercise of body, that plainness and frugality, which true wisdom leads to. . . if we know our wealth was collected in honesty, in equity, and in uprightness of heart, we may bestow it with God's blessing on those we leave behind us."

To those who had slaves, he argued, "Many slaves on this continent are oppressed and their cries have reached the ears of the Most High." He encouraged them to set their slaves free immediately, or, failing that, set them free in their wills (something George Washington would later do).

To all, he proclaimed that all men were created in God's image and deserving of freedom. "I believe that liberty is the natural right of all men equally." He also argued that free men would raise the standard of civilization higher than a society in which only half were free. "Free men, whose minds are properly on their business, find a satisfaction in improving, cultivating, and providing for their families; but slaves expect nothing but slavery and have no inducement to be industrious."

He considered leading a boycott against products created by slave labor, such as West Indies produce, but decided against it. "Were the trade from this continent to the West Indies to be stopped at once, I believe many there would suffer for the want of bread." Instead, he worked for the gradual, peaceful end of slavery.

One by one, Quaker meeting after Quaker meeting passed resolutions against slavery. Some even "read members out" of the meeting if they continued to hold slaves. These sentiments spread to the surrounding community, and by 1786 the New Jersey Legislature proclaimed: "The principles of justice and humanity require that the barbarous custom of bringing the unoffending Africans from their native country and connections into a state of slavery ought to be discontinued, and as soon as possible prevented." This same year, Quakers in New Jersey had virtually no slaves. Unfortunately, Woolman wasn't alive to see the results. He had died of smallpox while on a trip to England to convince fellow Quakers there to fight the slave trade.

Because of Woolman's actions, slavery died out in the north, and South Jersey would have many stations on the Underground Railway—in Salem, in Bridgeton, Greenwich, and Batsto. His tract, *Some Considerations on the Keeping of Negroes,* was the first important document in America to call for an end to slavery, while *The Journal of John Woolman* is considered a literary classic.

William Richards:
Ironmaster to a Nation

One of New Jersey's greatest colonial businessmen was William Richards. Ironworker, entrepreneur, patriot, owner of Batsto, Richards fathered 19 children and founded a New Jersey—and American—dynasty.

Richards was not a native New Jerseyan; he grew up on a farm in Berks County, Pennsylvania. A big boy, he worked hard next to his father, whom he adored. Like so many children in colonial days, he lost his father at an early age (the average life span in 1776 was 40 years).

His father's will stipulated that young Richards should "live with his mother for the space of one year, and then be put out to a trade which he liked." With no formal education except what he had learned from his mother, Richards chose to work at an ironworks when he turned 14.

One family story has it that he worked at the Coventry Iron Works, although years later he was more often associated with the Warwick Iron Works. While learning this trade, he fell in love with and married Mary Patrick of Pennsylvania. They were married in 1764 and their first child, Abigail, came in 1765. That same year, he showed his true patriot colors when he signed a petition opposing the British Parliament's Stamp Act.

Richards became associated with the Batsto Ironworks (near part of Wharton State Forest) for the first time when he took a job there in 1768. Winters were cold in those days, however, as the North Atlantic region was going through what climatologists call "The Little Ice Age." When ice froze the water wheel and halted the work, he returned to Warwick.

In 1773, he returned to Batsto to work as manager for owners John Cox and Charles Thomson. An advertisement published in 1773 confirms this position. Asking for the return of "two runaway Irishmen" (no doubt indentured servants), the advertisement is signed "William Richards, manager."

Unfortunately, whatever hopes Richards had for expanding Batsto and perhaps buying out the owners were temporarily dashed. On the horizon loomed dark war clouds—the war clouds of the American Revolution. In those years,

35

Batsto became indispensable to the Patriot cause, supplying George Washington with ammunition. After the war, Richards bought out his partners.

The specter of death was never far from Richards' house. In 1789, Richards' 3-year-old son died. In 1793, his eldest son John died. A year later, Abigail died, and not long after, his wife died. In 1797 and 1798, two more children died, and Richards even talked of selling Batsto.

He received new hope and energy, however, when in 1797 he married Margaretta Wood. She was 24. She gave him six children, including one named George Washington Richards and one born when Richards was 77.

In 1809, son Jesse took over the operation while William moved to Mt. Holly. Mt. Holly was less lovely than Batsto, but not as cosmopolitan as Philadelphia. It was perfectly suited to Richards' taste and needs, and his last years were apparently happy. He bought and sold real estate, donated land to St. Andrew's Episcopal Church, and retained his health and vigor right up until the end.

William Richards died in 1824, leaving an estate worth over $200,000. His greatest legacy was not his money, but his family—"human capital" that loomed large in the development of the Delaware Valley. From this river of a man flowed streams that affected nearly every area of American life. His descendents founded ironworks, glass furnaces, cotton mills, paper factories, and brick factories, employing hundreds of New Jerseyans and Pennsylvanians. They were lumbermen, merchants, inventors, and shipbuilders. Atlantic City was their brainchild, and they built the Camden and Atlantic Railroad to connect Philadelphia with Atlantic City. They established two of Philadelphia's largest banks, and one descendent became a mayor of Philadelphia. Three were members of the New Jersey legislature, and for years, the family was the largest landholder in the eastern United States.

Truly, William Richards deserves a place alongside the Astors, the Vanderbilts, the Rockefellers, and others. He founded a New Jersey—and an American —dynasty.

John Mathis: The Great One

One of South Jersey's greatest patriots was the "Great" John Mathis of what is now Ocean County. Although not a soldier himself, he provided invaluable aid to the American cause during the War of Independence.

Like so many other Americans, John Mathis came with his brother Charles to this country from England. In 1713, Mathis purchased the 250-acre Biddle Island (also known as Daniel Mathis Island) with partners William Birdsall and Moses Forman. The land was purchased from Daniel Leeds, New Jersey's first almanac publisher. In 1714, Mathis bought his two partners out, using his purchase to begin a land empire.

In 1716, Mathis married Alice Higbee, a young lady from another family that would become well-known in the annals of South Jersey history. Alice and John lived on Biddle Island until 1729, when Mathis bought 813 acres on the east side of Bass River. It was on this property that he built the place known as "the Great John Mathis House," for many years one of New Jersey's most historic houses. The house was located just a hundred feet from the Bass River Marina.

Like so many other South Jerseyans before and after, John Mathis turned his hand to shipbuilding. (On the eve of the Revolutionary War, the Delaware Valley, which included South Jersey, produced more ships than anywhere else in the country, including New England.) In fact, Mathis was the first to build a ship on Bass River. During the Revolution, he lent large sums of money to the fledgling U.S. government for the conduct of the war. Because of this patriotic contribution, he was referred to in official documents as "The Great John Mathis." The title, of course, was informal and honorary. History buffs from Ocean County continue to refer to Mathis as "the Great" in all references to him. Other contributions to the war effort by New Jerseyans included privateers and ammunition from Batsto.

After the revolution, the Continental Congress paid Mathis for his services in paper scrip, called Continentals, that were practically worthless (hence the phrase, "not worth a Continental"). For the next 7 years, Mathis would be land rich but cash poor. Only when the Constitution was adopted in 1787 and Alexander Hamilton's financial plan accepted would the value of the "Continental" rise again. These financial difficulties were part of the price Mathis and other patriots paid for founding a new nation.

Today, many people living in Ocean County trace their ancestry or land from the Great John Mathis. Relatives who made good include Thomas Mathews, one of the founders of Burlington, and a Matthews who was governor of Virginia.

John Mathis' Ocean County was originally part of Monmouth County. During the Revolution, it was a center of shipbuilding and privateering. Ocean County was created in 1850 (February 15) by an act of the New Jersey legislature. Little Egg Harbor Township, where Mathis once lived, was given to Ocean County in 1891 when the Democrats wanted to get rid of the Republican stronghold and gerrymander Burlington County, which became solidly Democratic.

Today, historians consider John Mathis to be one of Ocean County's greatest forebears.

BETSY ROSS
AND THE WOMEN OF THE REVOLUTION

Many historians discount the famous story that it was Betsy Ross who made the first American flag. One thing we learn from the study of history, however, is that there is usually some truth to any story that's been around long enough. Logically, the story's very existence means that we have to account for it somehow. The story is credible enough. We do know, for example, that there was a Betsy Griscom from Salem who married a John Ross. Because she was a Quaker and he was an Anglican, she was "read out" of the Monthly Meeting. Fortunately, both she and her new husband had marketable skills—they were apprentices in an upholstery shop. Moreover, Betsy had always shown a flair for art, and was known for her sewing ability and beautiful quilts.

John Ross, however, died early in their marriage, having been killed when an ammunition storehouse that he was guarding blew up. (A militiaman, he was one of the first casualties of the War of Independence.) The young widow was left to fend for herself. She worked harder than ever, even soliciting business from George Washington, sewing several shirt ruffles for him. Thus, when George Washington and Robert Morris, the "Financier of the Revolution," discussed a new flag with Colonel George Ross, Ross suggested that the stars be five-pointed rather than six-pointed and that they be arranged in a circle rather than scattered. A deal was struck, and Betsy Ross began making the first American flag. To help Ross better execute the project, the three men instructed her to visit a certain shipping company at the wharves, where she was given some old flags to see how they were made. Despite being an excellent seamstress, Betsy Ross had never made a flag before.

On June 14, 1777, Congress approved the flag, and the rest is history. Critics of this story say that Washington was so busy that he would have delegated the creation of a flag to others. Yet we do know that Washington could be a hands-on administrator, and that often there were too few subordinates to carry out his orders. (Remember that the country was young, with only 3 million people scattered from Maine to Georgia.) Moreover, the creation of a flag was no minor detail. All through history, flags carried great symbolism, and soldiers would fight to the death to keep an enemy from capturing the flag. So Washington certainly could have been involved in the decision to create a new flag.

Critics also point to the fact that the flag didn't come into widespread use until years later. This presents no problem because in those days, communication was slow and many colonies and regiments had their own flags It would naturally take some time for all fighting units to adopt the same flag. Historical records indicate that knowledge of the flag spread slowly. There is evidence to believe that the flag was flown over Philadelphia on July 4, 1777, the first anniversary of the Declaration of Independence. Ezra Stiles, later president of Yale, mentioned it in his diary in July of that year. In August, it was first mentioned in a newspaper. No matter who created that first flag, he or she would have faced the problem of getting the word out. There's nothing in this evidence that would take the credit from Betsy Ross.

Of course, Betsy Ross wasn't the only South Jersey woman to make an important contribution to the War of Independence. New Jersey seems to have had more women involved in the American Revolution than any other colony or state. Thousands of their names are not known to recorded history, yet these women played a critical role in winning the war. They nursed wounded men, tended farms while the men were away, bore sorrow, faced rape and pillage from the invading British, and saw their sons die untimely deaths (the majority of Washington's troops were teenagers). In a word, they made the Revolution possible.

For their part, New Jersey women were as well prepared for the war as they could be. Accustomed to rural and frontier life, most were muscular and inured to hardship. Women could hold some public offices, including sexton, jail-keeper, and public printer. In a frontier situation, men depended on their wives and often held their opinions and views in high regard. Widows commonly took charge of the family business when their husbands died. Eighteenth century newspapers carried advertisements from women who ran shops or taverns or owned mills or iron forges. In addition to gardening or farming, one of colonial women's greatest tasks was spinning cloth. Before and during the war, spinning was viewed as a patriotic activity. Women's associations in Salem County called on "patriotic females throughout the union to enter immediately upon the business of domestic manufacturers by plying the spinning wheel and the loom." Since cloth was Great Britain's most important export in the colonial era, the work of women directed to making America more self-sufficient was a form of economic warfare. Of course, women contributed to the economy in large measure, as they ran any business that had been left by the men going off to war.

Women also had to face the conditions brought about by the breakdown of law and order during the confusion of war. It was this kind of atmosphere that gave rise to the famous Joe Mulliner, the "Dancing Bandit." Mulliner and his

Photo is courtesy of The Betsy Ross House in Philadelphia, Pennsylvania.

band of about 30 men were supposedly loyal to King George III, but they were probably only loyal to themselves. Taking advantage of the fact that most able-bodied men were away, Mulliner would swoop down on an unprotected house, burning and pillaging without fear of reprisal. It was only after the war when the soldiers returned that Mulliner was captured and hanged.

Women were also active in raising funds to support the Continental Army. Indeed, they raised more than $15,000 within a few weeks in one year. During combat, women tended the wounded and carried water to swab the cannons. It was this last activity that gave rise to the legend of Molly Pitcher, also a New Jersey woman.

After the war, New Jersey gave women the right to vote, but only for a brief period. Like the rest of the country, New Jersey returned to the federal system under which each male voted as the representative of his family. Betsy Ross, who gave us a flag to follow, was one of many women who helped America attain its independence.

Phillip Vickers Fithian:
Leader of the 'Black Regiment'

Most people are familiar with the great love stories of Romeo and Juliet, Ivanhoe and Rowena, and Cinderella and her Prince Charming. But how about Phillip and Elizabeth Fithian? Their love story, set in historic Cumberland County during the American Revolution, is no less compelling, passionate, and tear jerking. And what is more, unlike the others, it is true.

Phillip Vickers Fithian was one of many colonial South Jerseyans who achieved national prominence. During the Revolutionary War, Fithian volunteered to serve as a chaplain in the Continental Army. But it wasn't for his patriotism that he made the history books. About a hundred years ago, his journals of life in Colonial America were discovered. As historians began studying his diaries, they were amazed at how well he described colonial life. When he traveled from New Jersey to Virginia, where he worked for awhile as a tutor, he found time to count, measure, or describe nearly everything in sight: the number of windows in each wall, the number of panes of glass in each window, the sizes of the out-buildings of a mansion, and the number of stays in a lady's dress. Indeed, so graphic were his descriptions that his journals were used extensively in the restoration of Colonial Williamsburg. Today, professional historians quote Fithian more than Confucius. But his journals also contain a record of his love life—his romance with Elizabeth Beatty, whom he called "that Vixen Laura."

Fithian grew up in Greenwich, Cumberland County, which he always referred to as "Cohansey" in his writing. The son of a pious farmer, he was sent to Princeton to study to be a minister under the able John Witherspoon. Returning to South Jersey, he met the beautiful Elizabeth Beatty in the parsonage of his former tutor, Reverend Enoch Green. It was love at first sight. They had everything in common, and talked for hours. When Elizabeth, whom he nicknamed "Laura," returned to her home in Pennsylvania, Fithian wrote to her: "For my part I cannot walk, nor read, nor talk, nor ride, nor sleep. . . I stand foremost in this gloomy row of the disappointed, for I saw you last of them all, and the transient golden minutes only fully persuaded me how much real happiness may be had in your Society."

For the next 6 years, while finishing his education at Princeton, then as a tutor in Virginia, he worshiped her from a distance. He wrote poems to her (later, he asked her to burn them, but fortunately, for the historians, she did not). He carved their names on trees. And he wrote letter after letter, expressing his love. Among the sweet nothings culled from his correspondence:

You are the person—the amiable object on which I have placed my esteem.
Such are you and I—made happy for a moment, made wretched by separation for months.
We are as near perfect contentment in each others company as mortals can come.

In his journals, he wrote: "In spite of all my strongest opposing efforts, my thoughts dwell on that Vixen Laura. . . like hidden fire they introduce themselves and seize and overcome me when I am at some useful or amusing study." Yet that didn't keep him from noticing the ladies in Virginia when he was a tutor in the home of Robert Carter. In his journals he complained of new dresses from London that have stays so high "that we have scarce any view at all of the ladies' snowy bosoms."

Despite the attractions of Virginia's southern belles, Fithian couldn't get his Elizabeth out of his mind. After spending 2 years as a teacher in Virginia, he returned to South Jersey and became a leading patriot and minister. In 1775, he participated in the Greenwich, Cumberland County, tea-burning protest against the British. He also preached at Pleasant Mills in Mullica Township, Port Republic, and Indian Mills.

Visiting Egg Harbor—the term used in those days to refer to Atlantic County —he gave one of the best descriptions of the region I've ever read. "There is something grand, charming and desirable in this vulgarly despised Egg Harbor. I love the simplicity which I see in the manner of the inhabitants. . . the country, the sand, the Pines. . . it is Nature stark naked."

Finally, that year, the one-sided romance became two-sided, as Laura returned his love and accepted his proposal of marriage. Before the year was out, they were husband and wife. Just before they were married, they had to be separated for a few weeks due to one of Fithian's preaching tours. Their parting was charged with emotion, as Fithian later described it: "She wept, and her powerful tears quite drowned me in melancholy rapture."

Sadly, like so many other young lovers on the eve of the American Revolution, their honeymoon was short-lived. Patriot that he was, Phillip volunteered for service as a chaplain in the Revolutionary Army. While ministering to the spiritual needs of the troops, he wrote of his next greatest love—America: "O America! with Reverence I look forward and view thee in distinguished Majesty —It is not rash to assert, without the aid of prophecy, that thy Commerce, and Wealth, and Power, are yet to rule the Globe!"

Photo of Tea-Burning Monument in Greenwich, New Jersey, is by Thomas H. Hogan, IV.

But Fithian's pen would soon lie silent. In 1776, in the service of his country, he became ill and died. It was a tragic end to a classic romance.

Whatever happened to Elizabeth? A few years later, she married Phillip's widower cousin, Joel Fithian. He was less passionate, maybe, but he was steady. They had four children, the oldest being named after Elizabeth's first love, Phillip. Joel eventually became a member of the New Jersey legislature. Phillip's last words to Elizabeth—"Peace and God's blessings be with my Betsy, my dear wife, forever may you be happy"—seemed to come true, at least outwardly.

Francis Hopkinson: He Signed the Declaration of Independence

From the south-central town of Bordentown came one of our most unusual signers of the Declaration of Independence, Francis Hopkinson. Even though he was considered a genius in his day—and the first truly American composer—"his head was no bigger than an apple" according to John Adams. Adams went on to say that "he was a pretty, little, curious, ingenious man; I have not met with anything in natural history more amusing and entertaining than his personal appearance, yet he is genteel and well-bred, and is very social."

Despite his small brain, he had big ideas. As is true in so many things, when it comes to the little gray cells quality is more important than quantity. Like Thomas Jefferson and Benjamin Franklin, he was interested in science and philosophy. He invented a shaded candlestick and an improved quill or "pick" for the harpsichord. He also designed the Great Seal of the State of New Jersey. He was a lawyer, musician, statesman, and businessman as well. After his birth in Philadelphia, his widowed mother went to great pains to give him and his siblings the best education possible. He was the first student to receive a diploma from the College of Philadelphia (now the University of Pennsylvania). Although he didn't take his first harpsichord lesson until he was 17, by age 20 he was giving successful public concerts. When he published *Psalm Tunes* in 1763, he became our first American composer.

In 1766, Hopkinson went to England, the land of his father, to seek a government appointment through the influence of relatives there. Among others, he visited the Bishop of Worcester, his mother's cousin; the artist Benjamin West, from whom he received instruction; and Lord North, a relative by marriage. But because the Stamp Act had been repealed, there were fewer jobs available, and Hopkinson returned home empty-handed.

On September 1, 1768, he married Ann Borden, the daughter of Colonel Joseph Borden, the leading citizen of Bordentown. Here he opened up a dry-goods store, where he sold imports from England. He grew tired of the merchant's life, however, and turned to law, which he had studied in college. Soon

Here is a depiction of Francis Hopkinson signing the Declaration of Independence.
(Artwork is courtesy of the Burlington County Library, New Jersey Room, Mount Holly.)

47

he was a leading lawyer in the Bordentown-Trenton area. In 1774, he was appointed a member of the Governor's Council; 2 years later, he was elected to the Continental Congress. Representing New Jersey in Congress, he signed the Declaration on "the Glorious Fourth." He was only 39 years old. As a signer, along with the others he pledged his life, his fortune, and his sacred honor. And like so many of the others, he paid a heavy price. The British marked him as a prominent rebel, and during the British occupation of Philadelphia, the Hessians were ordered to plunder his Bordentown house. His family barely escaped without injury or capture.

During the war, he served on various congressional committees and wrote songs and pamphlets to encourage his fellow Americans. During that time he composed his most famous poem, "The Ballad of the Kegs," in which he celebrates the early use of mines in warfare.

After the war, he became a district judge and became the first American to publish a complete *Book of Music*. He died of apoplexy in 1791, at the age of 54, but not before imparting a love of music to his son Joseph, who later became the finest harpsichord player in America, and was the author of "Hail, Columbia." Because of men like Francis Hopkinson, America won its bid to become an independent nation. His head may have been no bigger than an apple, but it was filled with ideas that helped get the nation through the crucial early years.

Joe Mulliner: He Danced His Way into a Hangman's Noose

Revolutionary War bandit Joe Mulliner's life is shrouded in legend. He is reported to have been tall and handsome, to have had a passion for elaborate uniforms, fancy swords, and pretty ladies. Some say he was a Robin Hood while others say he was little more than a highway robber.

Put all these stories together and what emerges is the leader of a gang of about 30 men who professed allegiance to the British crown, but who were actually only loyal to themselves. The confusion caused by the War for Independence, especially the fact that many of the men were away fighting in the war, gave Mulliner and his band of rogues the opportunity to pillage the Pine Barrens without fear of retribution. Working from a camp supposed to have been located on present-day Philadelphia Avenue in Egg Harbor City in Atlantic County, Mulliner and his band stole from local farmers and occasionally captured and held an important person for ransom.

One story about Joe Mulliner shows that even he could get disgusted with some of the things his followers did. One night, Mulliner's gang raided the farm of one Widow Bates, whose four older sons were serving in the Continental Army. Returning from church, the Widow Bates saw Mulliner's men leaving with most of her possessions. Undaunted, she gave them a tongue-lashing. "Silence madam," the leader is supposed to have said, "or we'll lay your house to ashes." "It would be an act worthy of cowardly curs like you," said the courageous Mrs. Bates.

The outlaws tied her to a tree, and as they had threatened, burned her house down. With typical old-fashioned South Jersey community spirit, Mrs. Bates' neighbors helped her rebuild the house over the next few weeks. But that is not the end of the story. Mulliner, it was reported, had no prior knowledge of the raid. Furious with his men and sympathetic with the Widow Bates, he supposedly sent her several hundred dollars' worth of coins.

Another legend has Mulliner (who loved to dance) breaking in on a party at the Kate Aylesford House and dancing with Kate Aylesford, while the rest of the guests were held at gunpoint by Mulliner's followers. The story is not true, since

49

there was no Kate Aylesford. (*Kate Aylesford* is the name of the first novel written in New Jersey history, by Charles Peterson. It centers on a fictional revolutionary heroine by the same name who frequented the Elijah Clark House near Batsto.)

It was Joe Mulliner's love of dancing that led to his downfall. One night, Mulliner was dancing and drinking at a tavern in New Columbia (now Nesco in Atlantic County). But South Jersey was no longer as safe for Mulliner as it had been. The Revolutionary War was over, and the men folk were back. In fact, an old Indian fighter named Captain Baylin had organized a company of rangers to capture Mulliner.

While Mulliner was dancing in Nesco, someone slipped out and contacted Captain Baylin. Mulliner doubtless could have danced all night, but Baylin showed up with enough rangers to disarm Mulliner's men and capture Mulliner. From Nesco, Mulliner was taken—with bound hands and feet—to Burlington, where he was tried, found guilty, and sentenced to be hanged. When his feet danced at the end of a rope a few months later, it would be his last dance. Now New Jersey was safe once again from that rascal Joe Mulliner.

CASIMIR PULASKI: THIS POLISH COUNT ONCE DEFENDED JERSEY

Contrary to what most people believe, South Jersey was not just the stomping ground of assorted Pineys, clam diggers, and pirates. From time to time, noblemen have visited and even lived here. It was the Polish nobleman and freedom fighter, Casimir Pulaski, for instance, who led American forces in repulsing a British attack in 1778. Sadly, the campaign was marred by the infamous Massacre at Little Egg Harbor, in which his outer guard was captured and killed. The wounded were given no quarter.

Pulaski had made it to South Jersey through an unusually circuitous route. He was born in Podolia, Poland, now part of the new nation of White Russia. In those days, there was no Poland at all—it had been gobbled up a few years before by the surrounding nations of Prussia, Russia, and the Austrian Empire. When he was just 20 years old, Pulaski became a leader of the Confederation of Bar, a patriotic revolt against the Russian occupation. The revolt was unsuccessful and Pulaski escaped to Turkey. From Turkey he went by sea to Italy, then north over the Alps to France.

It was in France that he met Ben Franklin, who induced him to use his military skill and experience in the service of the American colonies. With a letter of introduction from Franklin to General Washington, Pulaski arrived in Philadelphia. For distinguished service at the Battle of Brandywine, he was appointed chief of dragoons with the rank of brigadier general.

In 1778, he organized an independent corps of cavalry and light infantry, known as the Pulaski Legion. Expatriates like Pulaski, representing over seven nations, went into battle carrying a special flag of crimson silk made by the Moravian Sisterhood of Bethlehem, Pennsylvania (ironic, since most Moravians at the time were pacifists). It was this Legion that was called into action when the British attacked Chestnut Neck, now Port Republic. The British wanted to destroy this "nest of rebel pirates" as they called it and attack Batsto farther inland. Batsto was one of the chief armories of the Revolution. Count Casimir Pulaski and his hand-picked troops moved swiftly down from Trenton, too late to save

Chestnut Neck, but in time to pursue the British to Middle of the Shore, present-day Tuckerton.

In the early morning of October 14, 1778, Pulaski's outer pickets were surprised by a British attack. Outnumbered five to one, Pulaski's men had little chance, and even the wounded were bayoneted. Why were such experienced soldiers so easily surprised? It seems that a Hessian deserter, who had joined Pulaski, decided to switch sides again and let the British know exactly where Pulaski's men were encamped. Pulaski rushed to the scene, again too late. But he was able to chase the British away from Tuckerton, also a "nest of rebel pirates," as well as prevent the planned attack on Batsto. Batsto was thus preserved to continue to pour out munitions for the Revolution.

In 1950, the Ocean County Board of Freeholders erected a marker at the site of the 1778 massacre. It read, "The Pulaski Monument, commemorating the October 15, 1778 massacre commanded by Brigadier General The Count Casimir Pulaski of the Continental Army at Little Egg Harbor in the American Revolution."

Pulaski was later ordered to South Carolina, where he was involved in campaigns at Charleston and Savannah, Georgia. Pulaski commanded the French and American cavalry during the siege at Savannah, but was mortally wounded and died on October 11, 1779. With the death of Pulaski, the Pulaski Legion died as well. Today, his exploits are not forgotten, as scores of towns and other geographical units across the nation are named after him.

CHRISTOPHER LEAMING:
FOUNDER OF A SOUTH JERSEY DYNASTY

One of Cape May's first settlers was Christopher Leaming, whose descendants, among other things, compiled New Jersey's laws, included one of South Jersey's first millionaires, and were entrusted with the original Cape May Diamond by the king of the Lenape Indians. Today, Leaming's Run Gardens bears the name of this early New Jersey family.

Christopher Leaming left England in 1670, along with his brother Jeremiah, to seek his fortune in the New World. On the long and dangerous voyage, Jeremiah died, leaving only Christopher to carry the family name to America.

Christopher settled long enough in Long Island to marry Esther Burnet, whose father left them a trust of land later known as Leaming's Lot. Here they lived until 1691, when tales of whales and money to be made in Delaware Bay brought him to New Jersey's cape.

During the winter, Leaming hunted for whales. In 1693, for example, he got eight whales. Leaming spent the rest of the year following his trade of coffin and barrel making. There was plenty of demand for both—the barrels were needed to store whale oil, the coffins for the many who perished in the wilds of early America.

Unfortunately, as son Thomas later recorded in his diary, his father Christopher's arm became paralyzed for some unknown reason and remained that way until his death, putting a damper on all his activities. Leaming did, however, help to found Cape May's first permanent settlement, Town Bank. Here his remains were buried in 1697 when he died of pleurisy. (It is believed that this cemetery is now under water.)

Leaming didn't just leave behind a few barrels and coffins; he left behind his seven children, whose efforts would help to settle New Jersey's wild cape. Son Thomas made his own bricks and built a house in Cape May, where he brought his bride Hannah Whilden. Through this marriage, the Leamings trace their ancestry back to the Mayflower. (Hannah was the great-granddaughter of John Howland the Pilgrim. Due to this union, by 1920 one-third of all people in Cape May could

Christopher's son Thomas Leaming built this house on his father's property in Cape May in 1706. (Art is courtesy of Jack and Emily Aprill, proprietors of Leaming's Run Gardens.)

claim Pilgrim ancestry.) Christopher Leaming Jr. became an adventurer, participating in an invasion of Canada and working as a privateer off the New Jersey coast.

There were other well-known Leamings. Jeremiah Leaming, the sixth son, became an Anglican minister. Persecuted by his congregation during the Revolutionary War for his Tory sympathies (as an Anglican minister he was duty-bound to support the King), he was recalled to his pulpit by the same congregation after the war. Apparently they all decided to let bygones be bygones. Aaron Leaming settled in Goshen, becoming one of the state's leading cattlemen. In 1723 he became a justice of the peace, in 1727 a county clerk, and for 17 years served in the state legislature. In 1723, he purchased Stone Harbor and Avalon (Seven Mile Beach) for $2,500. For over 100 years, this island was known as Leaming's Beach.

Perhaps the most famous Leaming descendant was Aaron Leaming II, grandson of the original Christopher. Surveyor, author, lawyer, and legislator, he was the author of a diary which today is the basis of much of our knowledge of early New Jersey. Along with Jacob Spicer, he wrote a digest of all the early laws of New Jersey, known as the Leaming and Spicer Laws. He represented Cape May County in the state assembly for 30 years. At his death, his estate was found to be worth nearly a million dollars.

In the early 1800s, another Christopher Leaming, who had married Jacob Spicer's granddaughter, was given the original Cape May Diamond by King Nummy—last chief of the Lenapes—as a token of friendship.

Today, people can imagine what it was like to live in early Cape May by visiting Leaming's Run Botanical Gardens and Colonial Farm. A cabin built by Thomas Leaming is still standing there.

Patience Lovell Wright: America's First Sculptor

It took patience for America to bring forth its first bona fide sculptor—literally. Art historians tell us that Patience Lovell Wright (1725-1786) claims the distinction of being not only the first American sculptor but also really the only one of note during the Colonial period. And she was born right here in New Jersey.

Before Wright came along, the art of sculpture was purely functional: anonymous artists created such things as stone grave markers, metal weather vanes, and wooden figureheads. Decorative and often ingenious, these items are highly prized today. In colonial times, they were a practical necessity.

All that changed when Patience Lovell Wright came along. Born on Main Street in Bordentown, she was a Quaker and a niece of Methodist leader John Wesley. Little is known about her parents, but her sister, Rachel Lovell Wells, also became a sculptor. We can assume that the parents had some artistic or hand skills. After all, as the old saying goes, the apple doesn't fall far from the tree.

On March 20, 1748, Patience Lovell married a farmer, Joseph Wright, who died in 1769 after fathering four children: Joseph, Phoebe, Elizabeth, and Sarah. Like many artists, Wright discovered her talent quite by accident, to meet a need in her children's lives. To amuse little Joseph, Phoebe, Elizabeth, and Sarah, she began molding likenesses in bread dough and later in wax. So proficient did she become in wax that she moved to more cosmopolitan New York City to make wax statues. In June, 1771, her wax works were damaged by fire, causing several hundred dollars' worth of damage (a lot of money in those days).

As Wright's reputation grew, she decided to open a wax works in the heart of the British Empire: London. In England, she received international acclaim. Horace Walpole made mention of her in 1773, and the list of notables whom she depicted include Lord Chatham (the Cornwallis who was later defeated by Washington at Yorktown), Lord Lyttleton, and Thomas Penn.

Wright fit into London society well, despite her provincial upbringing in New Jersey. In fact, her daughter married the well-known English portrait-painter,

John Hoppner. Yet Wright was too much of a down-to-earth Jerseyan to let fame go to her head and cloud her judgement. When rumors of war reached her London wax works, she agreed to work as a spy for Benjamin Franklin. As the war dragged on, she went to Paris to help enlist the French support that would help us win the war.

During this period she also began busts of Ben Franklin and George Washington, but never completed them. She did make, however, a wax profile of Washington, probably from a clay bust created by her son Joseph.

Wright's work in wax included miniature profile portraits and complete busts. Her full-length effigy of William Pitt the Elder stood in Westminster Abbey. Ironically, many of the men she honored, including William Pitt the Elder and Admiral Howe, she also helped to defeat through her clandestine work with Ben Franklin.

Wright's work came to an end in 1786, when she died as a result of a fall while returning from a visit with John Adams, the American ambassador. At her death the famous American poet, Joel Barlow, recognized her greatness and wrote of her:

See Wrights' fair hands the lives her fire control,
In waxen forms she breathes the impassioned soul.

Today, New Jersey is not known as a center for sculpture, especially of busts of famous men and women. If you count the "sculpting," or carving, of famous ducks, however, we're second to none: there are more duckcarvers per square mile in the area from Barnegat Bay, Ocean County, to Cape May County than anywhere else in the world.

Richard Somers:
An Atlantic County Hero

New Jersey's sons and daughters have acquitted themselves well in defending their country. Near the top of the list has to be Atlantic County's Master Commandant Richard Somers, who gave his life at a critical moment in the history of our young Republic.

The son of an old New Jersey family—Somers Point takes its name from them —Richard Somers died a hero off the shores of Tripoli while engaged in conflict with the Barbary pirates.

Born on September 15, 1778, Somers was the son of Colonel Richard Somers. Young Richard grew strong working on his father's farm, Somerset Plantation, taking in the fine sea breezes amid pine forest air. On Sundays, neighbors met at his father's house where a Quaker meeting was held.

When he was old enough, he was sent to Burlington, New Jersey, for his formal education. In those days, Burlington was about as cosmopolitan as you could get for the colony of New Jersey. In addition to several inns, there was a motley collection of houses and cottage industries. Nearby, America's first Indian reservation struggled to survive. Ben Franklin had a printing shop there, and for one summer during the American Revolution, New Jersey's Provincial Congress had met there. Somers took advantage of the education offered at Burlington, as well as of the culture of nearby Philadelphia. At that time Philadelphia was the second largest city in the English-speaking world (London was first).

After Somers completed his education, he followed in the footsteps of so many other "Downjerseymen" and went to sea. In 1798 he received his warrant as a midshipman in the United States Navy. It was a young navy, but one which had already established its prowess by taking on the world's most powerful navy —the British. Somers and his shipmates—the heirs of John Paul Jones—were ready to take on all comers.

And comers there were: America was regarded as the new kid on the block, having no experience in a world of street-wise bullies. Thus, when the Barbary pirates in North Africa continued to attack and demand tribute from America's shippers, a confrontation was in the making. Other more powerful nations just paid the tribute. America, on the other hand, could ill afford the loss of prestige as well as money. President Jefferson's motto had been coined earlier by another great American, Charles Pinckney: "millions for defense, but not one penny for tribute."

It probably came as no surprise to Somers when he received a dispatch from Commodore Edward Preble, dated September 16, 1803. The dispatch read: "Sail immediately for Malaga, and take under convoy all the American merchant vessels bound to the westward and bring them into this bay. You are not to stay at Malaga longer than twenty-four hours. Should you fall in with armed vessels, of the Emperor of Morocco or, of his subjects, you are to bring them into this place for examination. . . " Earlier that year he had been given the command of the schooner *Nautilus*; now his mettle would be tested, perhaps in battle.

Somers successfully convoyed American ships in the Mediterranean, but still the Barbary pirates persisted in harassment. Eventually the U.S. Navy blockaded Tripoli Harbor, but it was Somers who came up with the plan to destroy the enemy's fleet, which was bottled up in the harbor. Somers and a crew of volunteers would sail a fire ship into the harbor and then explode it in the midst of the enemy's ships. All agreed that they would blow themselves up rather than be taken prisoner, if it came to that. The tricky part of the plan was that they would have to escape in a small boat before the explosion went off.

No one knows for sure what happened that night, but many scholars believe that the daring young man from Atlantic County and his crew stayed on board to insure that the explosion would take place. They went down with their ship, but the rest of the world was put on notice that Americans would protect their citizens anywhere in the world. The mouse had roared, and people were listening. To honor Somers, a grateful country named one of its ships the *U.S.S. Somers*.

An insight into Somers' character may be gained by reading a note he wrote to his closest friend, Stephen Decatur, another American patriot: "For yourself, dear Decatur, I have no words that I can write. To other men I may express my affection, and ask their forgiveness for any injury I have done them: between you and me there is nothing to forgive—only the remembrance of a brotherhood since we were boys."

Richard Somers—an officer, a gentleman, and a naval hero—was one of America's finest.

Jonathan Elmer: Jersey's First Senator

Jonathan Elmer, New Jersey's first senator, deserves to be considered a "Founding Father" right along with the best and brightest. Although he was no Washington or Jefferson, as a member of the second tier of Founding Fathers, he helped install the nuts and bolts of Washington and Jefferson's grand plans.

Born in Cedar Brook (Cedarville) in 1745, Elmer was a sickly child. But he overcame his early handicaps, received a classical education from his grandfather, Reverend Daniel Elmer, and Reverend William Ramsey, and went on to the University of Pennsylvania. At Penn, Elmer distinguished himself in medical studies and graduated in 1768 as a member of the first medical school class. His thesis was on fevers, dedicated to Penn's founder Ben Franklin and his son, William Franklin, then governor of New Jersey. In 1771, he received his doctorate.

Soon after, Dr. Elmer moved to Bridge Town, now Bridgeton, to set up his practice. Bridgeton was, after all, Cumberland's county seat as well as an important port. There he married Mary Seeley with whom he had eight children, four of whom died in infancy. Their house was located on the site of Bridgeton's present post office, on Broad Street.

Today, Bridgeton has the largest district of historic buildings in New Jersey, but, unfortunately, Dr. Elmer's historic house is not there. Just before it was demolished in 1926, a Bridgeton history buff, Carl Williams, wrote: "In the future the citizens of Bridgeton will regret the loss of this ancient house. It ought to have been preserved as a memorial to the man who lived and died in it."

In 1775, Elmer joined with his brother Matthew in publishing the first newspaper in New Jersey, *The Plain Dealer*. A year later, Jonathan read the Declaration of Independence to a public gathering at the County Court House.

Elmer had made his first foray into politics in 1772, when he was appointed Cumberland County Sheriff. As sheriff, he helped to foil the trial of the patriots who had participated in the Greenwich Tea Party. In 1775, he was appointed as a delegate to the Provincial Congress. From 1776 to 1789, he was the clerk of Cumberland County. But perhaps his greatest role at this time was as a congressman at the Continental Congress, where he served from 1776-78, 1781-84, 1787, and 1788. In 1787, he was also elected president of the Medical Society of New Jersey. He was a busy man.

In 1789, Elmer was chosen by the state legislature to represent New Jersey in the new Senate (in those days, senators were chosen by the legislature, not by the people). In the Senate, he developed a tremendous reputation for integrity —something many people are asking for today. One Senate colleague wrote of him: "I know not in the Senate a man, if I were to choose a friend, on whom I would cast the eye of confidence as soon as on this little doctor."

During Dr. Elmer's tenure as a U.S. senator, Bridgeton was made the official port of entry for most of South Jersey. Bridgeton retained this status until 1913.

Unfortunately, Dr. Elmer lost the support of many of his constituents when he supported the decision to locate the nation's capital in Washington, DC. Many of them viewed it as a sellout. Actually, it was a necessary and courageous compromise to get the Southern states to support Northern financial interests, measures that would benefit New Jersey. Today, Washington is closer to New Jersey than it is to most Southerners, or other Americans, for that matter. But people couldn't see that back in 1790.

In his politics, Elmer was a Federalist. That meant, generally speaking, he supported George Washington, he was pro-business, and he favored a strong central government (compared to the loose Articles of Confederation), and sought a lessening of tensions with England.

In 1793, Elmer returned to Bridgeton. His interest in politics began to translate into an interest in promoting Christianity. Specifically, his denomination was Presbyterian. He became a ruling elder in Bridgeton's Old Broad Street Church, a delegate to the General Assembly, and busied himself with evangelistic and benevolent work. He died on September 3, 1817. Patriot, politician, physician, and lay preacher—he was one of New Jersey's finest.

Joseph Napoleon: This King of Spain Once Lived in South Jersey

According to the United States Constitution, New Jerseyans—as well as other Americans—are not allowed to accept titles of nobility or royalty from foreign nations. We have, however, played host to various foreign dignitaries, including an ex-king, who became a resident of South Jersey. His name was Joseph Bonaparte.

In the early 1800's, the "Little Corporal," Napoleon Bonaparte of France, cast a giant shadow across Europe. While in power, he gave a number of his friends and relatives some of the fruits of his victories. To his brother Joseph, he gave the title of King of Spain. In those days, this was one of Europe's greatest crowns. The day when Spain was Mistress of the oceans and controlled colonies from South America to Africa was still fresh in people's minds. When Napoleon met his Waterloo and fell from power so did his brother Joseph, who now found that he was a man without crown or country. Joseph and his family left Spain post-haste, one step ahead of Spanish patriots, seeking refuge in Switzerland. He decided to book passage to the United States, accompanied by a secretary and disguised as an ordinary passenger. One suitcase of jewels was all he took with him, while the remainder he buried with his gold on the grounds of his Swiss refuge.

Upon his arrival in America, he looked for a place to stay, one that would measure up to his new social class; Bonaparte discovered Bordentown, just south of Trenton. Bonaparte decided to put down roots, and called his estate Point Breeze. Eventually, his property would consist of over 1,000 acres of forest with gardens and lawns. His home took 2 years to complete. When building was completed, he sent for his two daughters from Europe. Perhaps to protect against anti-Bonaparte assassins, Point Breeze had a tall outpost to overlook the countryside, as well as secret underground passageways. The tunnels were fortified with brick and were high enough for people to walk through standing erect.

To collect the rest of his Spanish fortune, (and presumably to pump some money into the local economy), Joseph sent his trusted friend and secretary, Louis Mailliard, back to the old country. Disguised as Stephen Girard, the wealthy Philadelphia businessman who founded Girard Bank and Girard College, Mailliard sailed from Philadelphia to Europe in 1817. He survived a shipwreck off the coast of Ireland, then made his way from Normandy to Switzerland. At Joseph's chateau in Switzerland, he found the ex-king's valet, Monsieur Veret. At midnight, they dug up the treasure. Jewels were placed in Mailliard's clothing, and the gold in trunks. Mailliard then headed to Brussels, Belgium.

In Brussels, Mailliard met with Joseph's wife, Queen Julie. Following doctor's orders not to travel, she decided not to come to America. But in Bordentown, Joseph was re-united with his other treasure, the jewels and gold, upon Mailliard's return.

Bonaparte never became a naturalized citizen, but the New Jersey Legislature passed a bill allowing him to own land, for all practical purposes making him a Jerseyman. Bonaparte lived in Bordentown for 14 years, and became somewhat of a local fixture. Among those who stopped at Point Breeze to pay their respects were John Quincy Adams, Henry Clay, and Daniel Webster. Bonaparte later traveled to Italy, where he died. Thus ended the story and life of a king of Spain who lived right here in South Jersey.

Art is courtesy of the Burlington County Library, New Jersey Room, Mt. Holly.

Charles Pitman: Famous Preacher

Early South Jersey was the domain of the circuit-riding preacher. Usually a Methodist, he preached one Sunday in one church, then rode horseback across the Pine Barrens to preach the next Sunday in another. Over a month's time, he would complete his "circuit," then start over.

Although a man of peace, the circuit-riding preacher was usually a rugged individual, braving inclement weather, poor roads, bandits, and working for little pay. The greatest of these itinerant evangelists has to be Charles Pitman, after whom the town of Pitman was named.

Charles Pitman was born in Cookstown in 1796, at the end of George Washington's second administration. His circumstances were modest: His father died in 1802, when Charles was only six, leaving his upbringing to his mother, Hannah Pitman.

Family and neighbors noted that Charles was a sensitive boy who liked poetry, song, and prose. Raised in a Methodist home, he was strongly influenced by Bishop Francis Asbury, who sometimes preached in nearby Pemberton.

By the time Pitman reached the age of 17, he was fully qualified—at least by 19th century standards—to be a teacher. Pitman took a teaching position at Cookstown, where he honed his already remarkable speaking abilities by lecturing to his students.

Walking 6 miles, both ways, to church every Sunday, Pitman gained a reputation as an earnest Christian. In 1816, Francis Asbury died, leaving the work in South Jersey to young Charles Pitman. He was licensed to preach at the age of 21 in 1817.

However, before the young preacher could get started, his life was marred by an all-too-frequent tragedy in those days—the death of his young wife in childbirth. Committing his son into the care of his mother, he threw himself into his ministerial duties. First he preached the Trenton Circuit, then in churches in the Philadelphia area where influential people began to notice his speaking abilities. His first full-time circuit was comprised of nine churches near Pennington. Later, he was moved to New Brunswick and later to Bridgeton.

64

Meanwhile, he married again and two more sons were born. All of these experiences and travels were giving him an intimate acquaintance for the land and people of South Jersey—uniquely fitting him for his next appointment as Presiding Elder over the District of West Jersey. (Back in those days West Jersey was essentially South Jersey, while East Jersey covered what is now North Jersey.)

In this supervisory position, Pitman traveled throughout the Pinelands, carrying with him hymnals, Bibles, and marriage certificates. He spoke frequently at camp meetings, often to overflowing crowds. Whenever he visited Pleasant Mills, for example, Pitman was entertained in the Batsto Mansion by Jesse Richards and his wife. (Richards is said to have esteemed and revered Pitman above all other men.) On one occasion, so many people showed up that the Pleasant Mills Church couldn't hold them, and Jesse Richards sent over a six-mule team wagon. Using the wagon as a platform, Pitman preached to nearly three thousand people standing in the churchyard.

When Pitman was later appointed to the East Jersey District, he became just as well-known in North Jersey. Subsequent assignments saw him serve as a fund-raiser for Dickinson College in Pennsylvania and as the Secretary of the New York Conference Missionary Society, for which he spoke widely on missions. In 1844, the University of North Carolina conferred on him an honorary doctorate. He was mostly self-taught.

In 1854, he retired to a home in Trenton. Worn out from the thousands of miles he had spent on horseback, Pitman wrote: "My nervous system is now so prostrated that my infirmities, if not my age, would make the weight of a grasshopper a burden."

That same year, Pitman passed away. A camp meeting ground in South Jersey was named Pitman Grove in his honor; this later became the town of Pitman. One of his sons went on to become a congressman from Pennsylvania. A Piney preacher, Charles Pitman helped to mold New Jersey's religious heritage.

Edgar Page Stites:
Famous Hymn Netted Him Ten Dollars

When people read of celebrities getting million dollar advances, the impression may be given that writers make lots of money. Nothing could be further from the truth. As my colleagues will tell you, there is not much money in writing, even in the writing of books. You have to love writing and what you write about. That's why it's important for writers to have other forms of income to subsidize their love of writing. Moreover, they need to have other interests so that their hearts don't get broken when their writing is rejected.

One of South Jersey's most famous writers, Edgar Page Stites, found all of the above to be true. For even though one of his hymns, "Simply Trusting," has been translated into hundreds of languages, he received only one dollar in payment for it. His most famous hymn, "Beulah Land," netted him only 10 dollars. His other poetic efforts were equally disappointing, at least financially. Providentially, Stites wasn't writing for money.

Born in Cape May on March 22, 1836, he grew up in the home of a Delaware River and Bay pilot, Page Stites. (The bay and river are so relatively shallow that pilots have always been necessary. Typically, pilots were picked up by seagoing vessels in Lewes, Delaware, or Cape May and left off in Wilmington or Philadelphia.) With water travel in his blood, he left home at age 15 and went to work for the Clyde Steamship Company. It was while he was in their employ that he wrote "Beulah Land," which was first read as a poem in 1876 at a Methodist preachers' meeting in Philadelphia.

In 1876, Philadelphia was arguably the most influential city in America. It was also the site of the nation's Centennial, when Egg Harbor City wines took first place in the vintners' contest. Concerning the poem, Bishop McCabe suggested to Stites that he submit it to Professor John Sweeney of Chester, Pennsylvania, a composer. Sweeney set the words to music, and within a few years it became the theme song for the evangelistic campaigns of Dwight L. Moody, the Billy Graham of the late 19th century.

Sweeney published the song in sheet music, and it was sold for as high as a dollar a sheet. He eventually made thousands of dollars from the sale, which was great for Sweeney, but Edgar Stites—or Edgar Page, as he sometimes signed his name—got only 10 dollars.

When "Uncle Joe Cannon," one of America's most famous and powerful Speakers of the House, visited Cape May (as had Henry Clay, Lincoln, and Ulysses S. Grant), Stites was asked to write a poem for him. After the poem was read, Cannon commented on the hymn "Beulah Land." "I'd rather have written Beulah Land," Cannon said, "than be elected President of the United States."

Stites was also known as a top-notch and avid fisherman. Indeed, it was probably while fishing that he came up with some of his ideas for his poems and hymns. Listening to the music of the ocean, to the birds and breezes in the tree tops, and looking out over the clouds across Delaware Bay and the ocean, his thoughts were turned often to heaven, or Beulah Land. And so he wrote "Oh, Beulah land, Oh Beulah land, I look away across the sea, where mansions are prepared for me."

Edgar Page Stites died at the age of 84 in Cape May, and was buried at the Old Brick Cemetery at Cold Spring with his *Mayflower* ancestors. (In the 1920s, two-thirds of all people living in Cape May were *Mayflower* descendants.) Although Stites was one of the most famous, there were other famous writers from South Jersey including Vineland hymn-writer Thomas Chisholm and novelist Charles Peterson, who wrote the *Kate Aylesford* novel.

Cape May's Captain Sawyer Sparked a Civil War Controversy

Much of South Jersey is technically below the famous Mason-Dixon Line, and in the election of 1860, New Jersey tilted towards the Democrats, who were strongest in the South. Nevertheless, when the Civil War began at Fort Sumter in 1861, the people of New Jersey rallied for the Union and organized their own units, including the First New Jersey Cavalry. Among these volunteers was Captain Henry Sawyer of Cape May. In 1863, Captain Sawyer became involved in a controversy that reached all the way to the White House and threatened to turn the Civil War into an even greater bloodbath, involving the wholesale massacre of prisoners on both sides.

In July 1863, Captain Sawyer was wounded in the thigh and neck at the Battle of Brandy Station. Left on the battlefield, he was taken prisoner by the Confederates. He was thrown into one of the most infamous jails in the South, Libby Prison in Richmond, Virginia. Sharing in his misery were 74 other Union officers. Their conditions were, of course, terrible. By 1863, the South had already lost the war (for all intents and purposes), and both Southern citizens and soldiers were suffering terribly. Many Confederate soldiers were fighting barefoot. As a result, there was little sympathy and even less material comfort for Northerners who had invaded the South. The North, for its part, had its share of infamous prisons, including Fort Delaware on Pea Patch Island, in Delaware Bay. (So many Confederate prisoners died there—over 2,700—that they had to row corpses to the mainland for burial.) As Captain Sawyer looked out of his dark cell into a fading Confederacy, he couldn't have imagined the byzantine trail of events that would soon involve him, a South Jersey boy from little Cape May, in a national controversy.

Confederate leaders decided that two Union officers held in Libby Prison would be executed in retaliation for the deaths of two Confederate officers on spy charges by Union forces. The two men chosen by lot to be shot were Captain Sawyer and Captain John Finn. Sawyer wrote a letter to his wife, living in Cape May, explaining his plight. Alarmed and outraged, Mrs. Sawyer took it to the media, and it was promptly published. Sawyer became a hero overnight.

Eventually, word of the coming execution reached Abraham Lincoln. Lincoln, who had vacationed in Cape May before the war, and was familiar with the town and its people, met with Mrs. Sawyer on July 14, 1863. Also present was Secretary of War Edwin McMasters Stanton. To save Captain Sawyer's life, Lincoln sent a personal letter to Robert E. Lee—possibly the most honorable man in the South. In the letter, Lincoln threatened to hang two Confederate officer-prisoners if Sawyer and Finn were hanged. Actually, they were the highest-ranking Southern officers in Union hands—General W. Lee and Captain Winder. Meanwhile, the *Richmond Examiner*, the leading paper in Virginia, fanned the flames of controversy by demanding swift execution of Sawyer and Finn. Lincoln's threat, however, caused Jefferson Davis to reconsider. As the weeks passed, other issues came to dominate people's minds, giving time for secret negotiations to take place.

In March 1864, a prisoner exchange was arranged that satisfied both sides. Finn and Sawyer were finally reunited with their families in Washington, DC. Sawyer built up his strength, then returned to duty with New Jersey's First Cavalry. His ordeal earned him the rank of major.

When General Lee surrendered to Ulysses S. Grant at Appomattox Courthouse in 1865, the war ended and Sawyer went home to Cape May. His hero status still intact, he was elected to the Cape May City Council. He also went into the hotel business. If he considered the "Libby House" as a possible name for his hotel, we'll never know. Suffice to say that his years in the Libby Prison taught him what good hospitality was not. Today, visitors to Captain Sawyer's Cape May can see one of the largest historic districts of Victorian houses in the nation, and dine in some of the region's top-ranked restaurants and inns.

CORNELIA HANCOCK:
SOUTH JERSEY'S ANGEL OF MERCY

Most Americans have heard of Dorothea Dix, the famous leader of Civil War nurses. But how about Cornelia Hancock of Salem County? Cornelia Hancock was our own version of the "lady with the lamp." Along with Clara Barton, Dix, Florence Nightingale, and others, Cornelia Hancock helped make nursing a respected profession.

Hancock almost didn't make it into the Union Army's ad hoc nurse's corps. As she explained in her autobiography, Miss Dix at first rejected her "on the score of youth and rosy cheeks." "It was considered improper for angels of mercy to appear otherwise than gray-haired and spectacled," Hancock added. But wounded men were dying so fast at Gettysburg, where she had applied, that Dix took her anyway.

Work began on July 6, 1863, when the 23-year-old Quaker girl entered a Gettysburg church. The pews were draped with the dead and dying. With no formal training, no medicine, and no supplies, Cornelia reached into her own inner reserves of strength, kindness, and resourcefulness. She wrote letters for soldiers whose fingers had been blown away. A pious Quaker opposed to alcohol and tobacco, Hancock would, nevertheless, roll and light cigarettes for men whose arms were but stumps. When she found a wagonload of brandy, she used it to clean wounds and ease pain. She heard the prayers of men who wouldn't last the night. She did whatever she could to keep men alive who had been through the horrors of war.

Her description of the battlefield is a powerful antidote for anyone who thinks war is grand. "The deadly, nauseating atmosphere robbed the battlefield of its glory, the survivors of their victory, and the wounded of what little chance of life was left to them," she wrote.

A slight woman—only 5 feet tall with blue eyes and silken hair—she truly must have appeared as an angel to men who hadn't seen their mothers, wives, or sweethearts for months at a time. So much did the soldiers in the Gettysburg hospital revere her that later that summer, they had a medal struck in her honor, as "a testimonial of regard for ministrations of mercy to the wounded soldiers at Gettysburg, Pennsylvania."

In the fall of 1863, Cornelia visited South Jersey, but later that year could be found in Washington working with freed slaves. In 1864, Secretary of War Stanton gave her a pass to go anywhere in the lines of the Union Army. Eventually, the First Division Band composed "The Hancock Gallop" in her honor. She met both President Lincoln and General Grant, and achieved national fame.

Of all the soldiers she attended, one in particular, Frederick Dudley, stood out in her mind. They corresponded and friends thought they might marry after the war. But when the war ended, so did the mention of Dudley's name in Cornelia's letters. No one knows who broke off the relationship, but when Cornelia died, a packet of letters was found in her nightstand. Next to the packet was a note reading, "Burn without reading." The letters perished, and with it any hope of finding out what passed between Cornelia and Frederick.

Cornelia's later years were spent working with freed slaves, helping them to assimilate into American society and enterprise. Hancock died in Atlantic City. New Jersey's own angel of mercy, Cornelia Hancock helped lay the foundation for the modern profession of nursing.

Dr. Jonathan Pitney: Father of Atlantic City

On a bright May day in 1820, 23-year-old Jonathan Pitney dropped his saddle-bags in front of Hannah Holmes Tavern in Absecon and announced he was opening a practice on the edge of the Pine Barrens. Eventually, Dr. Pitney would not only become the area's most prominent citizen, but "the Father of Atlantic City."

Born in 1797 in Menham, Morris County, Pitney left the rolling hills of his birthplace to settle among the sand dunes, pines, and marshes. In this sparsely populated region, his practice soon stretched all across Atlantic County.

In between treating patients (a typical treatment included calomel, julep, and sweet nitre) he found time to get involved in civic affairs. He became postmaster and a recorder of shipwrecks. In 1835, he joined his voice with those calling for a new county to be created out of old Gloucester County. Dr. Pitney—along with many others since 1785—believed that Gloucester was too big and the seat of government too far away to be responsible for the shore's oyster-men, salt-makers, and charcoal-burners. Leading the charge for separation, Pitney got the Gloucester County Board of Freeholders to resolve that a division "would greatly promote the convenience and the interest of all sections of the county." After a 2-year debate, Atlantic County was finally created, on February 7, 1837, with Atlantic taking 613 square miles from Gloucester, and Gloucester giving $6,947.75 to Atlantic as its share of public buildings. Dr. Pitney was chosen first Director of Atlantic County's Board of Freeholders. By this time, Pitney held over 500 acres near Elwood.

In 1844, Pitney represented Atlantic County in the State Constitutional Convention, while in 1848 he was an unsuccessful candidate for Congress. But it would not be for politics or medicine that Dr. Pitney would be chiefly remembered. Pitney admired the rugged beauty of Absecon Island across the bay, and often went there for healthful walks along the shore. In 1845, while walking there with Absecon lumber mill owner Gen. Enoch Doughty, he turned and exclaimed, "This could become the El Dorado of the Atlantic Coast, Enoch."

Pitney wasn't thinking of gold, which was part of the original legendary El Dorado, but of a place where city dwellers could come and be renewed by the sea air and water. Here, in a spa-like atmosphere, people could get away from the hustle and bustle of the 19th century city.

Long before, the Lenape Indians had the benefits of summering at the shore, making the trek from the Delaware River each year to enjoy life on what they called Absegami, or "little sea water." In 1825, one observer described Absegami or Absecon Island as an area of sand hills filled with quail, rabbit, foxes, terrapins, wild fowl, minks, muskrats, and snakes. Other features included scrub pines, holly, bayberry, and cedar groves. Small creeks cut through from the ocean and the bay, and salt-water ponds filled the low areas. On some dunes, beach grasses were 50 feet high.

Pitney began his campaign by writing to Philadelphia newspapers, promoting the area as a health resort. Soon many doctors in Philadelphia came to agree with him. He then enlisted the support of South Jersey businessmen and landowners Thomas, Samuel and Jesse Richards; Joseph Porter; William Coffin and Andrew Hay; William Fleming; Stephen Colwell; and his close friend General Enoch Doughty. Together they proposed a railroad from Camden to Absecon Island; they hoped that the closeness to Philadelphia would draw visitors away from Cape May, then the nation's premier resort.

Meeting in John Doughty's Absecon store, Pitney and Enoch Doughty drew up the first charter for the railroad, only to see it rejected. But Pitney was a man who refused to take no for an answer, and in 1852, when they applied again at Trenton, the charter was approved. The powerful Camden and Amboy Railroad, which could have blocked it, never dreamed that a railroad to the shore could be successful. The railroad was completed in 1854.

All that was needed now was a name for the health resort, which engineer Richard Osborne supplied when he wrote "Atlantic City" across a map. The name became official on March 3, 1854, when the incorporation papers were signed. On May 1, 1854, 18 of the 21 eligible voters elected Chalkley S. Leeds Atlantic City's first mayor. It was only fair, since out of the seven houses on Absecon Island, four were owned by the Leeds' family.

Pitney's last great service to the area was to obtain a lighthouse for the island. As a recorder of shipwrecks, he had recorded one death too many. As early as 1840, he had requested of Congress and the Navy that a lighthouse be built. Congress first approved the idea, but then refused when Commodore La Vallette of the Navy Department made an unfavorable report. But Dr. Pitney wouldn't give up. He circulated petitions, wrote Congress, and published articles in newspapers. Finally, Congress appropriated $35,000 for a lighthouse, which was first illuminated in January 1857.

CHARLES LANDIS:
BULLISH ON SOUTH JERSEY

Landis Avenue, which begins outside of Vineland, New Jersey, and runs for more than 10 miles, is one of the most beautiful streets in New Jersey. On the outskirts of town, Landis Avenue is lined with prosperous-looking, well-kept farms. In town, stately homes are set back from a tree-lined avenue. But even more interesting than this well-known boulevard is the man after whom it was named: Charles Kline Landis, the founder of modern Hammonton, Vineland, Landisville, and Sea Isle City, New Jersey.

Like many Americans, Landis came from a family that had suffered persecution in Europe and fled to America for religious freedom. One of his ancestors, John Landis, had been found guilty of heresy by the Inquisition and was beheaded in the year 1600. Before his execution, however, he fathered three sons—all of whom escaped to the New World. The Landis brothers located in Bucks and Lancaster Counties, Pennsylvania. It was from this clan that Charles Landis was born, on March 16, 1833, to be exact, and lived intermittently in Philadelphia and Macon and Atlanta, Georgia. In those days, the Civil War hadn't yet poisoned relations between North and South, and there was free movement of people across the Mason-Dixon Line.

Educated at home and by private tutors, Landis was apprenticed to a lawyer and was admitted to the bar in 1852. But a career in law wasn't as lucrative as it is today. People tended to settle their own disputes. Wills were drawn up by the local minister or schoolteacher. Government was so small that there was little need for lawyers to help people wade through red tape. Accordingly, lawyers often had to find some other business to supplement their incomes. Landis chose real estate.

By 1856, Landis was so involved in real estate that he gave up his law business to form a partnership with Richard J. Byrnes, a young banker from Philadelphia. Their goal was to develop the lands around Hammonton, New Jersey. In those days, Hammonton was known as a center of glassmaking and had a regional post office. Soon Landis and Byrnes put together a substantial parcel of

Art of Charles Landis is courtesy of The Vineland Historical Society in Vineland.

land around Hammonton by making purchases from the Richards, Chews, Peterson, and Cooper families, as well as from Charlotte Cushman, a prominent actress. Landis and Byrnes then divided the land into small parcels and advertised them in newspapers all along the East Coast. Aided by the railroad, which was completed in 1854, Hammonton soon became a success.

But Landis had even bigger plans. In 1861, on the eve of the Civil War, he dissolved his partnership with Byrnes and put together a parcel of 32,000 acres of land in Cumberland County. On August 8, 1861, he felled the first tree, thus bringing into existence the city of Vineland.

Before Landis began promoting Vineland, he wanted to make sure that settlers moving in would have essential services. Accordingly, he cut a road through the woods, opened a post office, and began publishing a newspaper, the *Vineland Rural.* His idea of making wide streets, especially Landis Avenue, was a stroke of genius, and made it easier for Vineland to move into the Age of the Automobile.

Landis was particularly interested in making Vineland an agricultural center, especially for grapes, hence the name Vineland. Landis envisioned miles of truck farms that could supply the big eastern cities. In order to make this dream a reality, he began advertising for Italian workers. Landis believed that Italians were excellent fruit and vegetable farmers, and would help to put Vineland on the map. Subsequent history showed that he was right, and soon Italians came to own most of the farms around Vineland.

In the midst of all this activity, Landis found time to begin two other South Jersey communities, Landisville (of course) and Sea Isle City. In Sea Isle, Landis saw to it that a Life Saving Station was set up to assist seamen lost in shipwrecks along the Jersey coast. On October 14, 1868, Landis had married Clara F. Meade, niece of General George C. Meade.

Charles Landis died on June 12, 1900, leaving behind at least four South Jersey communities as his legacy.

P. M. Wolsieffer:
Father of German Music in America

Egg Harbor City is a small town in the Pine Barrens of New Jersey. On the surface, it looks like any other small American town. Scratch the surface, though, and you'll find a heritage as German as sauerkraut and Wiener schnitzel. There are streets still bearing the names of Beethoven, Duerer, and Mozart. What's more, the first mayor of the town was the "Father of German Music in America," Phillip Mathias Wolsieffer.

Wolsieffer was born in Winwieler, a city in the Rhenish Palatinate, in 1808. Born at the same time as Abraham Lincoln, Wolsieffer's life would take a different turn than Lincoln's. Whereas Lincoln grew up on the frontier, and then later went to the city, Wolsieffer grew up in civilization and later became a pioneer.

Wolsieffer immigrated to the United States in 1833, and was a music teacher for a while in New Haven, Connecticut. He then moved to Philadelphia, and then to Baltimore. Baltimore at mid-19th century had a large German population, and later many from this town would come to Egg Harbor. It was here that Wolsieffer founded what was probably the first German musical society in the United States. For this reason, Wolsieffer is known as the "Father of German Music in America."

Wolsieffer's involvement with Egg Harbor commenced in 1854 when he became secretary of the Gloucester Town and Farm Association, which had been formed by a number of prominent Germans to establish a German settlement in Egg Harbor. Wolsieffer came to Egg Harbor as one of the first settlers and planted a vineyard. In those days, Egg Harbor was a nationally known project, designed to give refuge to 100,000 Germans who were facing the anti-immigrant prejudice of the Know-Nothing Movement.

Trunks of felled trees were still lying around in the pioneer settlement when Wolsieffer founded the Aurora Singing Society in June 1857. This society survived well into the 20th century, and for six decades remained the most popular and most respected social organization in town. The Aurora Singing Society brightened the routine of pioneer life with concerts and theatrical performances.

P. M. Wolsieffer conducted the Aurora Singing Society here at Aurora Hotel in Egg Harbor.
(Photo is courtesy of Robert A. Peterson.)

Not yet condemned to television, the people of early Egg Harbor responded enthusiastically to the productions of the Aurora. Wolsieffer served as the Aurora's first conductor.

His peers must have respected Wolsieffer, for on June 8, 1858, he was elected the first mayor of Egg Harbor. Wolsieffer continued his career in statesmanship, and in 1866 he was elected by the people of Egg Harbor and the surrounding areas to serve in the New Jersey legislature. In those days, Egg Harbor was something of an anomaly, as it was the only city in the state to conduct its town meetings completely in German. The city clerk had to write the minutes completely in English as well as in German, however, for the convenience of state and other civic authorities.

Wolsieffer left Egg Harbor sometime after 1867, and spent most of the rest of his days in Philadelphia. Phillip Mathias Wolsieffer left his mark as Egg Harbor's first mayor, and as the "Father of German Music in America."

Salvatore Calabrese: He Founded a Little Italy in South Jersey

Today, Hammonton, New Jersey, is well-known for its Italian-American heritage. It still has some of the best Italian-style meat and produce markets and restaurants in the area. Italian is taught in the high school, and some residents still keep in contact with the "blueberry Capital of the World." But it wasn't always that way. In fact, Hammonton's first settlers were transplanted New Englanders who were *Mayflower* descendents. They were sturdy, serious-minded Yankees. All that would change, however, with the coming of Salvatore Calabrasi (Calabrese, hereafter).

Salvatore Calabrese was a Civil War veteran, having fought in the Union Navy. Wounded in battle, he had been honorably discharged. Arriving in Hammonton in 1863, he bought property on Pine Road. Because there were virtually no other Italians in the area, Calabrese married a girl of German descent, Caroline Schwartz. When two other Italians, Mattia Campanella and Antonio Capelli, passed through in 1866, they heard a fellow countryman was there and sought him out. (The 1850 census had turned up only 3,645 Italians in all of America.) Four years later, 19-year-old Domenico Campanella, brother of Mattia, arrived. Soon a steady stream of letters flowed back to their boyhood home in Gesso, Sicily, telling relatives of the veritable Eden they had found in Hammonton. Eventually, over a period of three decades, the whole town of Gesso would pick itself up and move, forming a Little Italy in southern New Jersey.

There is no reason to wonder why so many Italians wanted to come to Hammonton and America. Although years of warfare and revolution had forged an Italian nation by 1870, people were weary of the machinations of Count Camillo de Cavour, the revolution in Sicily, even the heroics of freedom fighters like Guiseppe Garibaldi, which drained the manpower of Italy. In Gesso, Sicily, things were even worse. Gesso was an old town, its terraced soil having been depleted by long-vanquished civilizations. Yet absentee landlords demanded that the tenant farmers, the Contadini, produce a good crop from the barren soil. Other residents had no work at all, yet faced the salt tax and high prices for bread. The

Messina area was also subject to severe earthquakes. Earlier in the century, over 70,000 lives had been lost due to earthquakes.

The government—the Kingdom of the Two Sicilies up to 1870 and a united Italy thereafter—offered little protection and no services for the people. Some turned to the Mafia, while others chose a different path, pursuing the promise of America. So many came to America that Gesso became the "mother of Hammonton." Some of the first families to arrive included the Vuottos, the Persicos, Tomasellos, Tells, DeStephanos, Lucos, Petreccas, Pintos, and Saccos. The Reverend N. Walling Clark, head of educational work for the Methodist Church in Italy, said of such families, "The southern Italians will work tirelessly once you have earned their trust." And work hard they did, for they brought little with them. In fact, historians estimate that the average immigrant arrived with $17.14 in his pocket—the equivalent of 2 weeks' wages for an unskilled worker in the United States. They faced prejudice at first. For a time, all the jokes were about Italians; while working on their citizenship, they were called "Wops," or people without papers. In time, they became fully assimilated into the population, though their contributions live on in many areas. Such contributions include family and religion; community pride, based perhaps on the Italian village concept, or paese; one of the world's most varied cuisines, and historical and artistic traditions that date back to the days of the Roman Empire.

Unfortunately, Mr. Calabrese did not live to see the full blossoming of Hammonton as New Jersey's "Little Italy." He died at the age of 42 on August 1, 1881, just when the influx of immigrants was beginning to pick up momentum. But he died a highly respected man in the community. His funeral at the Presbyterian Church was filled to capacity, attended by the newly formed Masonic Society, and presided over by the Baptist minister. He was then buried in a Methodist Cemetery in the town of Winslow. Mrs. Calabrese, on the other hand, lived until 1941, when she died at the age of 95. In her long lifetime she had seen Hammonton change from a community of transplanted New Englanders to one of the most Italian-American cities in America.

Colonel John McKee:
Founder of McKee City

He was a colorful figure: a restaurant owner, a land baron, a colonel in the Pennsylvania National Guard, a philanthropist, educator, civic leader, and the founder of McKee City. His name was Colonel John McKee.

Born in Alexandria, Virginia, in 1821, McKee was a freeman in a time that offered little opportunity for African-Americans. At the age of 21, he moved north to seek his fortune in the city of Philadelphia. It was a wise choice: Dominated by a Quaker evangelical Christian ethos, Philadelphia had long been known to offer more opportunities for African-Americans than most towns in the north.

McKee opened a restaurant located at Eighth and Market Streets. The operation must have been profitable, for a few years later he bought a block of row houses and began collecting rent. Meanwhile, McKee joined the Pennsylvania militia and began rising through the ranks. Eventually, he became the first African-American colonel in the Pennsylvania National Guard.

As his wealth grew, so did his vision for two special projects: a large estate devoted to farming and a military college, both for orphans of all ethnic backgrounds. The first desire may have been motivated by a desire to help those like himself raise themselves up by their bootstraps. In the South, the majority of African-Americans were in slavery while those in the North were tenant farmers on lands owned by whites. McKee realized that if African-Americans were to gain political power, they had to have economic power—not black power, or white power, but "green" power. Finally, he was a businessman who wanted to increase his own holdings.

By the time McKee was able to act on the first part of his plan, the Civil War had taken place. Slavery was over, but not poverty for both whites and blacks. Thus, in 1884, he began buying land in Atlantic County in Hamilton and Egg Harbor Townships. McKee, like Charles Landis in Vineland and the German founders of Egg Harbor, laid out the streets himself. He constructed his own sawmill and used the lumber cut there to build saltbox houses.

81

Although McKee spent much of his time in the colony, he still lived in Philadelphia. Once every 2 weeks he would take a train to McKee City and then rent a horse and buggy from one Michael Hopkins and tour his lands. Parcels were rented out to tenants with the idea that they could eventually earn enough to buy a farm. McKee insisted that the area be called "McKee City" on all documents and the name endured.

McKee's second vision, that of a college for orphans, was probably inspired by Girard College in Philadelphia. Girard College had been founded for male orphans a few years before McKee arrived in Philadelphia. Girard was financed by the estate of Stephen Girard, a wealthy banker and financier. McKee's new college was to be a military one, with an iron statue of McKee astride a horse. McKee made provisions for the college in his will, but after McKee died, it was found that there was not enough money to carry out the project. Instead, a scholarship fund was set up for needy students in the Philadelphia area.

Upon McKee's death it was discovered that he also had extensive land holdings in West Virginia, Georgia, and Kentucky. How he obtained the money to amass such an empire is not known.

Today, McKee City is the location of the Atlantic City Racetrack, Hamilton Mall, and an expanding collection of businesses and homes.

Dr. James Still:
'Black Doctor of the Pines'

One of the greatest African-Americans in New Jersey history is Dr. James Still, the celebrated "Black Doctor of the Pines." Raised in abject poverty, and having little more than 6 months' schooling, Dr. Still became a legend in his own time, healing "Pineys" of all ethnic backgrounds in an area far from city doctors and hospitals. But Still was more than a doctor; he was a businessman, an author, a scientist, and, in one sense, even a preacher.

Born in 1812 at Indian Mills in Burlington County, James Still was the son of escaped slaves Levin and Charity Still. As a boy, Still was bound out to labor in the fields of Amos Wilkins, a nearby farmer. In his spare time, he chopped wood with his father and sold firewood. One of the hazards of the job was that, in those days, bears roamed freely over the Pine Barrens. "I remember when three of them passed through my father's field," he later wrote in his autobiography.

Still's father was a strong, religious man whose strictness helped the younger Still bridle his passions and channel his limitless energy towards good ends. At the age of 19, Still managed to spend about 6 months in school, only to be asked to leave by a teacher who had "come to the conclusion" that "blacks should not study with whites." Ironically, that teacher's name is forgotten—like the ghost towns of the Pine Barrens—while Still's name is respected in many circles in America today.

At the age of 21, Still left the Pines to seek his fortune in Philadelphia, where he took a job in a glue factory. Although he worked 12-14 hours a day, he would still return home to read more books, just as Ben Franklin had done in the same city a century before. He also memorized Latin medical terms and increased his knowledge of botany.

City life didn't appeal to Still; after 2 years he returned home to the Pines, a land of pine boughs, sphagnum moss, and cedar swamps. Back in New Jersey, Still met a young girl, Angelina Willow. "I learned four love songs, and sung them every day until I got married, and have not sung them since," he later wrote. James and Angelina were married on July 25, 1835. The following winter, the weather was so bad the Stills had an imposed honeymoon. On one occasion the snow fell for 3 days, and drifted so high that normal work and travel was impeded for 5 weeks.

Tragically, Still's young wife died shortly thereafter. Their baby daughter, Beulah, was given to Still's mother to raise. Stunned by the loss of his wife, Still underwent a spiritual experience that changed him forever; he became, as he put it, a true Christian. "I then joined the church," he wrote. "Previous to this I had fears of thunderstorms, but all fears were dispelled in my new trust in the Lord Jesus." Still soon remarried the former Henrietta Thomas who was originally from Vincentown. "One thing we had in abundance," he said, "and that was poverty." But with hard work and frugality, Still slowly built up his medical practice, and invested the profits in lands and buildings.

Often Still's remedies would consist of mixtures of natural ingredients collected from the forests; other times it was simply his insight into human nature and his positive outlook on life. On one occasion, he was called to Mary Sooy's house. When he arrived, everyone, including Mary, told him that she was dying. Still took her by the hand, felt her pulse, looked her in the eyes and said, "Miss Sooy, you are not dying, and will not die this time. I know that you and everyone must die sometime, but you will not die now." Using this approach, Still was able to help Mary get back into good health within a few weeks. It was a case of the will to live, spurred on by Dr. Still, triumphing over a defeatist attitude.

Jealous of Still's success, several doctors took him to court for giving out prescriptions without a license. A lawyer cleared the matter up by pointing out that although there was indeed a law against giving prescriptions, there was no law against selling and delivering medicine. Still thus went on selling and delivering medicine with his usual down-home bedside manner.

By dint of hard work and careful management, Still acquired quite a bit of property in Burlington County. Although he suffered a mild stroke in later years, he spent the rest of his life tending the sick who would flock to his office. In 1877, he wrote an autobiography entitled *Early Recollections and Life of Dr. James Still*. Available from the Atlantic County Library, it ought to be required reading in New Jersey history courses.

In his autobiography, Still gives the secret of his success; his advice is good for anyone:

All men like the esteem of their fellows, and this may be brought about by energy, honesty, and upright deportment. Shun the society of the lewd; there is nothing to be gained from them but vice and poverty. Do not allow yourself to be enticed to the gambling house, where the mind becomes dwarfed and hardened against what is good and great... Treat all men with decorum. Be assiduous in all your undertakings. Fulfill your promises to the letter. Read instructive books, among which the Bible is

Art is courtesy of the Burlington County Library, New Jersey Room, in Mount Holly.

first. Be unassuming in your manners. Turn a deaf ear to those who call you a fool for your pains, and discourage you from attainment. Press forward, the prize is before you and for you."

With these words and through his actions, Dr. James Still remains before us as one of our finest New Jersey role models.

Dr. William Newell:
Victorian Lifeguard

One of the first and undoubtedly most famous "lifeguards" in New Jersey history was Dr. William Newell of Ocean County. No, Dr. Newell wasn't a strapping young man with a golden tan and blonde hair, but he was instrumental in inventing the first "lifeline" and establishing the first government-supported lifesaving stations. His efforts eventually formed the basis of what later became the U.S. Coast Guard.

Dr. Newell's crusade to make the coastline safer began on a summer night on Long Beach Island in 1839. Fresh out of medical school, Newell was walking on the beach in the midst of a summer storm when he saw the Austrian brig *Count Ferasto* break up on a sand bar only 300 yards from shore. Trained to save lives, Dr. Newell rushed to the water's edge and out into the breakers to try to help. But soon the cries for help—in German and other East European languages—grew silent. All that the sea gave up were 14 lifeless bodies.

Returning home to Manahawkin, Newell found that he could not concentrate on his medical practice. The vision of 14 men dying just 300 yards from where he was standing—and his own helplessness—continued to haunt him.

But Dr. Newell wasn't about to go "off the deep end." He began experimenting with what he called a lifeline, which would be shot out to ships by means of a shortened blunderbuss, or mortar gun. The ship would then be towed to safety by means of the lifeline.

But a lifeline was no good if there were no lifesaving stations or teams to launch such a line. So Newell decided to run for Congress, where he could aid the still relatively young nation in developing a U.S. Lifesaving Service. In 1846, Newell won his first term to Congress, representing the Second District, which stretched from Sandy Hook to Little Egg Harbor. Year after year, he pushed to establish a Lifesaving Service. Year after year, it was defeated. But each year, the number of sponsors grew. Finally, in 1855, he succeeded in attaching an amendment to the Senate Lighthouse Bill when it came to the House. The bill provided for surfboats, carronades, and other safety equipment to be established along the shore to aid in preventing shipwrecks. A total of $10,000 was voted to fund the new organization. As the program proved its worth, Newell was vindicated, and the Lifesaving Service was expanded. Stations were set up from Little Egg Harbor to Cape May and north toward Long Island, New York.

Recognizing both his foresight and his achievements in making the coastline safer for New Jerseyans and other Americans, President Lincoln appointed Newell superintendent of the Lifesaving Service. In fact, Lincoln came to respect Newell so much that he was appointed Lincoln's personal physician. In 1865, he returned to New Jersey and was elected governor. But that was not all. A few years later, President Hayes appointed Newell governor of the Washington Territory. He was the only New Jersey man to serve as governor of two states.

And what of his Lifesaving Service? As originally written in Newell's Bill, the duties of the Lifesaving Service included the protection of life and property along the shore. The Revenue Cutter Service, another Federal program, protected the coast and enforced customs regulations. The services were finally combined on January 28, 1915, forming the modern day U.S. Coast Guard.

More perhaps than anyone else, New Jersey's own William Newell deserves the title of "Father of the U.S. Coast Guard." And it all began on a lonely beach on Long Beach Island, back in 1839.

Thomas Welch: He Invented the Nation's First Bottled Fruit Juice

Throughout history, many important discoveries or advances came about as a result of Bible study. The inventor of anesthesia, for example, had read of how God put Adam to sleep so that one of his ribs could be taken out and a woman formed. The discoverer of ocean currents, Matthew Fontaine Maury, had been inspired by Psalm 8, which pronounced that there were "paths in the sea." Today, a river in Virginia is named after him and he is honored as "the Pathfinder of the Seas." Even Christopher Columbus was encouraged by what Bible scholars and monks told him about the Earth: It was indeed round, according to Isaiah 40:22, where the words "circle of the earth" mean "sphere" in Hebrew.

Welch's Grape Juice, started in South Jersey, came about in a similar manner. In the spring of 1869, Vineland dentist Dr. Thomas Bramwell Welch was elected Recording Steward of the Vineland Methodist Church. A strong prohibitionist (like many of Vineland's founders), Welch objected to his election on the ground that he could not in good conscience provide fermented wine for the Communion service. (Hadn't the Bible warned its readers "not to be drunk with wine but to be filled with the Holy Spirit"?) Rev. A. K. Street's reply was, "Well, you are elected and you can provide whatever you please." Having just read about the theories of Louis Pasteur, Welch wondered if they could be applied to making grape juice that wouldn't ferment. So, with his wife and 17-year-old son Charles he picked about 40 pounds of concord grapes, squeezed and seeded them, boiled them long enough to kill all the yeast organisms, and bottled the juice.

For weeks the family waited, listening for the explosion that would signify failure. But no explosion came. Dr. Welch had succeeded. His own Methodist Church was the first to use the pasteurized grape juice but soon many others followed. Thus was born the nation's first bottled fruit juice, which, along with fruit-flavored bottled iced tea, is currently one of the hottest items in the food and beverage market.

Eventually, demand for the product became so great that Welch and his son Charles, also a dentist, gave up their practice to devote full attention to grape juice sales. For the younger Welch, this paid off in more ways than one: In 1879, the records show he sold 12 pints of grape juice to a Jennie Ross of Burlington, New Jersey. A year later, he married her.

In 1896, Dr. Charles Welch began moving his operations to the large grape growing areas of western New York State. Two factors that influenced this move were that Welch felt that he had outgrown Vineland, and the grape-rot had destroyed much of South Jersey's vineyards.

About this time, Charles Welch embarked on one of the nation's first countrywide advertising campaigns. He advertised in the *Ladies Home Journal, Scientific American*, and many other magazines. Welch's was served at the St. Louis Fair and the Chicago Exhibition, and was promoted by the Temperance Movement as the only nonalcoholic fruit drink on the market. And when Woodrow Wilson's Secretary of State, William Jennings Bryan, held a dinner for the British ambassador and Welch's was served instead of wine, Welch's Grape Juice became a household phrase.

The following year, the Secretary of the Navy, Josephus Daniels, forbade the serving of the Navy's rum ration and ordered Welch's in its place. People poked fun at the order, inventing the slogans, "the Grape Juice Navy" and "Give'm Grapes, Josephus." But the more the decision was criticized, the higher the volume of sales. Other products were added, including Welch's Grape Jelly. Today, Welch's is still the name people think of first when referring to grape juice.

In addition to Charles, Thomas Bramwell Welch had seven children, several of whom became dentists, including a daughter. Born in England in 1825, he had immigrated to the United States with his parents in 1834. Originally trained as a minister, he became a doctor when his voice failed. Further health problems caused him to limit his medical activities to dentistry. Dr. Welch died in 1903 in Philadelphia.

Welch's Grape Juice is just another example of the influence of religion and resourceful men on our nation's history. Both are an important part of New Jersey's heritage.

Photo of Dr. Thomas B. Welch is courtesy of Welch's, now based in Concord, Massachusetts.

George Washington Pressey:
He Invented the First Safe Bicycle

The first bicycle was invented in 1816, yet by the mid-1800s the bicycle was still a dangerous contraption. With a big wheel in the front (for speed) and a small one in the back (for balance), riders were easily thrown over the handlebars of the bike when they hit a rock.

Enter transplanted New Englander George Washington Pressey of Hammonton, a town nestled deep in the Jersey Pines. With the success of his "American Star" bicycle, Pressey's name became a household word in 19th century America. Today, Pressey's bicycle stands in the Smithsonian Institute next to early models of the Haynes and Ford automobiles.

Pressey grew up in Maine and moved to Hammonton in 1860. The son of a carriage maker, he had already established himself as an inventor, developing the first apple paring machine, a carriage spring, and new carriage tools. In 1866, the year Hammonton got its charter, Pressey was respected enough to be elected tax assessor and served as one of the original directors of the Hammonton Loan and Building Association. But paperwork and meetings couldn't quench his inventive spirit. New inventions that flowed from his fertile mind included the Pioneer Stump Puller, the Pressey Folding Umbrella, and a ventilating stove. His invention of a Pressey Brooder for the brooding and artificial hatching of chicks caused him to go into the poultry business and helped make New Jersey one of the leading poultry-producing states.

It was in 1881 that Pressey's most enduring invention appeared—the American Star bicycle. The new thing about the Star was that the front and back wheels were reversed, with the large wheel in the back and the small in the front. The result was a much safer bike, as the rider was less likely to pitch forward over the small wheel. This may be difficult to envision without a picture, as most people today only ride bikes with wheels of equal size. But old-timers say that it really was safer.

To prove the bike's worth, Pressey's son Burt entered races in Massachusetts and Philadelphia, beating all other entrants. In 1882, he rode down the steps of the Capitol in the presence of government officials to prove the bike's safety.

To mass-produce the bike, Pressey took his idea to Hezekiah Smith, who had a furniture factory in Smithville, near Mt. Holly. Smith liked the idea, and South Jersey became a center of bicycle manufacturing.

But that's not the end of the story. In order to get his workers from Mt. Holly to Smithville, Pressey's friend Smith developed a bicycle railway. Completed in 1892, it was a rail upon which bicycles moved. The trip took little time as bicycles went as fast as 18 miles per hour.

The late 1800s became the great age of bicycle makers. People rode bikes to go to the new soda fountains that were popping up in every small town, and with their best girl or guy on Sunday afternoons. The Wright Brothers, who built the first airplane, were actually bicycle makers. Bicycle makers were thus on the cutting edge of turn-of-the-century technology. George Washington Pressey and the American Star—they're both a part of our rich New Jersey heritage.

Joseph Campbell:
His Soups Were M'm! M'm! Good!

Often in history one great achievement leads to another. Sir Isaac Newton, the great English scientist, discoverer of gravity, once said, "If I have seen further than others, it is because I have stood on the shoulders of giants."

In South Jersey history, one such giant was Colonel Robert Gibbon Johnson of Salem. According to legend, Johnson was the first white man to eat a tomato and survive. The real story goes something like this: Johnson, one of New Jersey's first scientific farmers, knew that tomatoes were not poisonous. Unfortunately, even as late as the 1800s, many New Jerseyans wouldn't touch a tomato, thinking that it could cause serious illness or even death. Johnson changed all that by mounting the steps of the Court House in Salem and eating three fresh tomatoes. Needless to say, he lived.

Of course, people had been eating tomatoes—in Latin America—for years. But it is historically true that for most of the 18th century and well into the 19th century, most North Americans believed that tomatoes were poisonous.

Johnson's bold act, as well as those of other South Jerseyans whose names never got into the history books, paved the way for another milestone, the founding of the Campbell Soup Company. For it was with the tomato that Joseph Campbell first put his canning company on the corporate map in the late 19th century.

Joseph Campbell was born on the outskirts of Bridgeton, Cumberland County, May 15, 1817, the son of James and Hannah Campbell. The fruit and vegetable industry was in his blood. His father was a devout Presbyterian who sought to live by the dictates of Scripture, and was a successful fruit farmer. Joseph Campbell eventually left the farm to work as a purchasing agent for a Philadelphia company.

In the early 1860s, just as the first shots of the Civil War were being fired, Campbell joined with Abraham Anderson to found a canning factory in Camden. Anderson and Campbell soon developed a reputation for excellent canned fruit and vegetables. Their best product was (you guessed it) canned tomatoes. Or perhaps we should say canned tomato, for the celebrated beefsteak tomato

94

Photo of Joseph Campbell is courtesy of the Campbell Soup Company in Camden.

was so large that only one was packed to a can. Other canned products included canned peas, corn, mince meat, jams, jellies, and apple butter.

In 1876, Joseph Campbell and Abraham Anderson parted ways. Anderson wanted to rest on the laurels of the past, while Campbell wanted to expand. The company has been expanding ever since.

After operating his canning factory alone for about 7 years, Campbell brought in his son-in-law, Walter Spackman, in 1881. Spackman, in turn, introduced Campbell to Arthur Dorrance, whose name is still associated with the company.

The turning point in the company's history came in 1897, when Joseph Campbell reluctantly hired Arthur Dorrance. Dorrance was a fine young man, but he had one major liability: He had too much education. In addition to a degree in chemical engineering from MIT, he also held a Ph.D. from the University of Gottengen, Germany. And as everyone knew at the turn-of-the-century, a college education often dulled a man's ability to do real work. Dorrance was hired, nonetheless, with the stipulation that he finance the outfitting of his own lab. It was one of Campbell and Dorrance's greatest decisions, as Dorrance went on to invent condensed soup. And, yes, one of the first and most popular was tomato soup.

On March 27, 1900, Joseph Campbell suffered a heart attack and died at the age of 83. Until the day he died, Campbell took the train daily from Riverton to Camden to inspect his business.

Today, Campbell's legacy lives on in what is one of the world's largest food processing companies. The Campbell Soup Company owns companies such as Pepperidge Farm, Vlasic, Mrs. Paul's, Prego, and many other brands. The Campbell line includes more than 1,000 items sold in the United States and 120 foreign markets. And it all began with a Jersey farm boy, Joseph Campbell.

INDIAN ANN:
LAST OF THE INDIAN MILLS LENAPES

The Lenape Indians, although always small in number, left an abiding legacy in the South Jersey area. Place names like Tuckahoe (where the deer are shy), Atsion (Indians nearby), Rancocas (many kinsmen), Cinnaminson (sweet waters), and Pennsauken (crooked river) all come from the Algonquin language. The White Horse Pike was named after Chief White Horse, while Nummy Island, Nummy Town, and Nummy Trail were named after one of the last kings of the Lenapes. Indian Mills was the nickname for the first Indian reservation in America.

The Lenapes also left a legacy of peace with the early settlers. Wilted Grass, the Lenape leader who handled the final negotiations of the Indian Mills reservation with the state of New Jersey, wrote this letter of thanks to the New Jersey legislature: "Not a drop of our blood have you spilled in battle; not an acre of our land have you taken but by our consent. These facts speak for themselves and need no comment. They place the character of New Jersey in bold relief, a bright example to those states within whose territorial limits our brothers still remain."

Although the Lenapes left the reservation in 1832 to move to Wisconsin, one Indian would remain behind to keep their legacy alive. We know her as Indian Ann. Although much of her story is legend, here is what historians have been able to piece together. Indian Ann was a basket weaver in Indian Mills, Tabernacle Township, Burlington County. Ann was of average height and build and wore her long black hair in braids. Normally, she wore the typical shirtwaist housedress popular in the 1800s. But unlike most 19th century women, she liked to smoke a pipe. According to reports, she usually could be seen with a clay pipe in her mouth.

For her livelihood, Indian Ann made straw baskets of various sizes and shapes and sold them to locals and passers-by. She would also carry a basket to bring home items that people gave her or that she gained in barter. One of the legends of Indian Mills is that Indian Ann would never go home with an empty basket. If a housewife had just baked, she might receive a loaf of fresh bread. If a farmer had just butchered a hog, he might put in a piece of pork. Her philosophy was: "another day, another dollar," or as Longfellow put it more eloquently: "Each morning sees some task begin, Each evening sees its close; Something attempted, something done, Has earned a night's repose." She left us with a good economic lesson that we should always try to bring home more than we spend on any given day. Locals also say that she had a clock that had to be wound each day with an iron key. Afraid she might damage something in the clock, she would usually ask someone else to wind it for her.

The daughter of Chief Lasha Tamar, she was born on the Woolman farm near Rancocas in 1805. Her father had lived in New York for a time with a Lenape colony there. She was married twice. Her first husband was Peter Green, a former slave. Her second husband was John Roberts, another freeman who lived with Ann in a small frame house on Dingletown Road near Indian Mills. Here Indian Ann reared seven children: Peter, John, Samuel, Richard, Hester, Ann, and Lydia.

During the Civil War, John Roberts volunteered to serve with the 22nd Regiment of Colored Troops. He enlisted in December 1863. Unfortunately, he was either wounded in action or fell ill and died in an army hospital at Yorktown, Virginia, on February 17, 1864. Sixteen years later, Indian Ann applied for a pension, something that Civil War veterans had fought for and won in Congress. At first she was given $8 a month; in 1886, it was raised to $12 a month.

In her 80s, Ann lived on the pension and proceeds from basket sales and picking wild berries. By now, she was part of the local landscape, a familiar figure on the road between Vincentown and Mt. Holly. She died in December of 1894, a professing Christian, and was buried in the Methodist Cemetery in Tabernacle. Eventually, her gravesite was upgraded by the Burlington County Historical Society. With the death of Indian Ann, so went one of the last of the Lenape Indians, certainly of those who had lived at Indian Mills, and certainly one of the most colorful.

ᴀNDREW ᴩIDER:
KING OF THE CRANBERRY BOGS

The next time you enjoy a glass of cranberry juice or a side of cranberry sauce, thank Andrew Rider of Hammonton. Andrew Rider was my kind of man: Trained to be a scholar and university president, he gave up the scholarly life to grow and promote the lowly New Jersey cranberry.

Born in Howell, Michigan, on March 12, 1843, Rider was graduated from the Bryant-Stratton Business College of Chicago. Distinguishing himself as a fine student, he was hired by the college to work in its New Jersey branch in Newark. From Newark, he was sent to manage the Trenton campus of Bryant-Stratton. Under Rider's leadership, the school became known as Trenton Business College. It became Rider-Moore Business College in 1898 and finally Rider College in 1921.

While in Trenton, Rider took an interest in South Jersey, which was just beginning to develop. In 1889, he bought a small bog near Hammonton to cultivate cranberries, and built a beautiful home on Bellevue Avenue 10 years later. So captivated was he by the cranberry that he eventually increased his holdings to more than 500 acres. Unfortunately, the virtues of the cranberry were little known in the 1800s. It had no aroma, as did strawberries, and was not sweet, like blueberries. Neither did anyone realize how good cranberry juice was for the kidneys. About the only sure market was among sailors, who popped cranberries like vitamin Cs to prevent scurvy.

Andrew Rider decided to change all that. In 1898, he threw off his regalia and resigned as president of Rider College. He would devote the rest of his life to promoting the cranberry. In Rider's day—as in our own—Americans were interested in everything that British royalty did. If Prince Albert put up a Christmas tree, as he did, then Americans would follow suit. And if British royalty ate cranberries, Rider figured, so would Americans.

In 1893, Rider set out on a British luxury liner, taking with him many crates of cranberries. Rider took only the best berries (berries that "bounced" when dropped). For as old "Pegleg" John Webb of Ocean County had discovered, bad

Photo of Andrew J. Rider is courtesy of Rider University in Lawrenceville.

berries don't bounce. Indeed, if they are rotten they plop. On the voyage, Rider ate, slept, and drank cranberries. He even talked the head chef into making cranberry sauce for the passengers. And on his lapel, there was always a bouquet of cranberries.

When he reached England, Rider found that although cranberries were well known, they were not liked—mostly because of the unsatisfactory way in which

100

they were prepared. In order to improve the situation, Rider published a *Cranberry Cookbook* and gave it free-of-charge to English restaurants. But the clincher was when the horse he bought, which had been named Cranberry, was a winner at Ascot. This resulted in an invitation from the Prince of Wales to send a crate to his residence. Eventually, some cranberry dishes found their way to Queen Victoria's dinner table. Her response was "Tell Mr. Rider that I liked the berries from Hammonton."

By the time Rider left England to sail back to South Jersey, England was importing 5,000 barrels of cranberries a year. Rider had put Hammonton and the New Jersey cranberry on the map. In his day, New Jersey produced half the nation's supply.

Rider spent his last years helping to build the town of Hammonton. He helped found the Hammonton Telephone and Telegraph Company, the Hammonton Trust Company, and the Hammonton Shade Tree Commission.

As an interesting sidenote, in the course of running his cranberry business, Rider became involved in a murder case that received national attention. Rider, his brother Henry, his daughter Mrs. Elsie Smathers, and John Rigby were driving out to Hampton near Atsion on Route 206 with a $4,000 payroll to pay their cranberry pickers, or "scoopers." While traveling through the woods, they found their way blocked by eight gun-wielding men. When the car didn't stop, all eight men started to fire. Rider pulled out a pistol and returned fire. Meanwhile, his sister stepped on the gas and got out of range. Unfortunately, Henry Rider had been killed.

In time, as the famous Burlington County detective Ellis Parker unraveled the case, it was discovered that among the eight men was one of Rider's workers who knew about the payroll. Eventually, all eight men were identified. One was caught, tried, and executed. Italian authorities captured another and gave him life in prison. Another was killed in a gang fight in Newark. Still another was captured in Pennsylvania, and the fifth was found in California serving a prison sentence. The other three were never found. They may have died or fled the country. Such was the state of justice at the turn of the century, when men were still held responsible for their actions.

Andrew Rider, the "Cranberry King," as he was called, died in Hammonton, January 14, 1929, at the age of 85.

John Wanamaker: King of Merchants Helped Develop South Jersey

For over a hundred years, the John Wanamaker store in Center City Philadelphia was a regional institution. Like Marshall Fields, Wanamaker was a pioneer in developing the department store. Each Christmas, people from around the Delaware Valley, including South Jersey, would take the train or drive by car to see what new seasonal display Wanamaker's designers had dreamed up. A registered national historic landmark, his store had the world's largest organ, the eagle statue from the 1904 World's Fair, a six-story atrium, the Crystal Tea Room, and a free art gallery. The building remains, but the business has been sold and the name changed. Yet the Philadelphia legacy remains, and part of that legacy is Wanamaker's work in developing southern New Jersey.

Born in 1839 in Philadelphia, Wanamaker was the son of a poor brick-maker. His first job, as a boy, was to turn bricks over to help them dry in the sun. His mother wanted him to be a minister, but after much prayer and hard thought he felt he could serve God just as well in the business world. The basis of his philosophy was Christian concern for the individual. If people were treated kindly and fairly, they would patronize your business, and both customer and businessman would be served.

He opened his first store on the eve of the Civil War on Sixth and Market, where the Liberty Bell is now on display. He applied to join the Union Army, but was rejected for health reasons—a persistent cough. By 1876, he was looking for a new location, and settled on Thirteenth and Market, where his store would stand for the next 100 years and become a Philadelphia landmark. Construction of the new store was delayed, however, when Wanamaker agreed to let evangelist Dwight L. Moody use the site (the old freight station) for a series of meetings. The Billy Graham of his day, Moody preached to thousands of people over 2 months. Wanamaker, a dedicated Christian, paid Moody's expenses and entertained him in his home. Because of the delay, Wanamaker lost thousands of dollars in business, but gained in public relations: After the meetings, everyone in Philadelphia knew where the new Wanamaker store was going to be.

Wanamaker didn't support Moody for pecuniary reasons; he was merely successful at integrating his religious and business lives. Years later, he would always close his business on Sundays and was so opposed to Sunday newspapers that he tried to buy a paper that had started a Sunday edition. He also had an excellent collection of Easter paintings but refrained from exhibiting them because he "didn't want to take advantage of religion."

Wanamaker didn't invent the department store, but he took the concept further along than anyone else did. As a boy, he had tried to return something, but the owner said he had to keep it even if he didn't want it. Wanamaker vowed that such a thing would never happen in one of his stores. He also ended the practice of haggling. He thought every customer should know exactly what he or she would have to pay for an item, and not have to haggle over the price. He also had a knack for advertising, and believed that advertising reduces prices because it creates a mass market. For many years, his advertising supported the existence of several Philadelphia newspapers. Another innovation, his in-store eatery eventually became the largest restaurant in Philadelphia. Meanwhile, he obtained the world's largest organ from the 1904 St. Louis World's Fair and sponsored free organ concerts for the public. He also put an art gallery in every store. The pictures were to be enjoyed, not bought or sold. He felt an obligation to bring culture into the daily commerce of peoples' lives; otherwise, they might not have a chance to see beautiful things or hear good music. Because of his marketing acumen, sales at his store went through the roof. On one occasion, he sold 223 pianos, 185 rugs, and 573 bicycles all in one day.

Wanamaker also pioneered many of the employee benefits that some corporations are now cutting. He believed that his best assets walked out of the store each day; they were his employees. If someone left the firm, he felt it was his fault. In order to make them stay, he added an employee lunch counter, a health and fitness center, and a health clinic to his store. In one year, his doctor and nurse gave over 46,000 treatments in the infirmary. And by 1911, on the roof of the Wanamaker building was an athletic field, a track, a promenade, two tennis courts, and two volleyball courts where employees could go and unwind.

It was Wanamaker's interest in benefits for his employees that led to his interest in South Jersey. He founded, for example, Camp Wanamaker on Barnegat Bay so that the city boys and girls who worked for him could get 2 weeks' free vacation. This wonderful benefit took lower income young people away from the sweltering heat of Philadelphia to enjoy the seaside and good moral instruction.

An even bigger project was Sea Grove at Cape May Point. Sea Grove was to be a religious resort much like Ocean City in the early days or Ocean Grove in central New Jersey. The first thing to be constructed was a pavilion. Next came the Sea Grove Hotel as well as a number of smaller hotels and boarding houses. To encourage people to come, Wanamaker offered several inducements. Lots valued at $500 were offered for free to clergymen or for congregations wishing to build summer homes for their pastors. Free passes on the West Jersey Railroad were offered to each new cottage owner. Wanamaker himself built a home there, and took up a collection from wealthy friends to build a summer home for President Benjamin Harrison. Wanamaker, who by this time was serving a 4-year stint as Postmaster General of the United States, presented the key of the completed house to the First Lady at the White House. This area later became the town of Cape May Point; many of the original buildings have been destroyed by fire or by sea. The pavilion was dismantled, and the Sea Grove Hotel became a summer retreat for the Sisters of St. Joseph. Today, narrow streets radiate from the circle where the pavilion once stood.

Wanamaker was always ready with a wise saying that he attributed ultimately to the Bible, such as "A little more effort on the part of everybody to make times better, and better times will surely come along." Or this: "You mend your automobile on the spot when something is broken; don't let your life go on with something broken in it either." Two other well-known sayings (Wanagrams, as they were called) are: "If you want things done, call on busy men because a man of leisure has no time," and "Men are great as they are kind." Today, there are no longer any Wanamaker stores, but the value of his contributions in opening parts of South Jersey as resort areas cannot be denied.

Walter Scott Lenox: America's Master Potter

For years, Lenox China in Atlantic County has been the nation's leading china maker. It is the largest company of its kind in America, producing fine china that is sold all over the world. But just who or what was Lenox?

Born in 1859, Walter Scott Lenox grew up in Trenton, which was at that time the center of American pottery production. As a boy, he wanted to be an artist and, after completing an apprenticeship in pottery, devoted himself to mastering design and decoration. In his 20s, he became art director of Trenton's Ott and Brewer Factory.

Lenox's creative genius and high aspirations were limited, however, by the demands of the American marketplace. A pottery firm could succeed only if it sold practical pieces at low prices, since the more expensive china services were bought from abroad. Most Americans who could afford fine china felt that America simply could not produce beautiful china. Designs and trends were set in Europe, just as patterns for American fashion were later set in Paris. But Lenox would change all that by making American china so exquisite that a demand would be created for it.

In order for such a vision to become reality, Lenox took his savings of $4,000 and formed a partnership with Jon Coxon; the business was called the Ceramic Art Company. Because Lenox was trying to create the world's best china, the early years were not profitable ones. On one occasion, he watched his workmen remove $2,000 worth of china, only to notice that there was a tiny, almost imperceptible flaw in every piece. He turned to the workmen and told them to throw everything into the junk heap. During these years, his financial backers were so sure he would fail that they insisted his factory be designed so it could easily be converted into a tenement building.

Even though he went blind and became partially paralyzed in 1895, he refused to give up the quest to create fine American china. Little by little, the china he produced began to attract the attention of the American public. His first big break came in the early 1900s when Tiffany's of New York put one of his services on display and became a regular customer. By this time, his partner had dropped out and the company was known as Lenox, Inc.

But the big break came in 1917, when President Woodrow Wilson—who, as a former governor of New Jersey, knew Trenton and its industries—ordered a 1,700-piece dinner set costing $16,000 from Lenox. It was the first American-made china to be used in the White House. Since that time, Presidents Franklin D. Roosevelt, Harry S. Truman, and Ronald Reagan have turned to Lenox to supplement the White House china set. In 1919, Lenox was able to burn all his mortgages and operate in the black. He died a year later.

Since Walter Scott Lenox's death, the company has continued his exacting standards in both making fine china and meeting the needs of its customers. One set of china was decorated to match perfectly the red hat of the late Cardinal Spellman; another was created for a desert prince who wanted to set a table for over 1,000 guests. One millionaire who wanted service plates decorated with pheasants commissioned a party of Lenox artists to travel around the world and sketch pheasants. The job was completed and today the plates are considered priceless.

In recent years, Lenox has met the needs of American consumers by selling china services in separate pieces. Over a period of time, it is possible to put together a china service that only the rich could once afford.

In 1940, Lenox sales were near 1 million; today, it's a multimillion dollar enterprise, owned by Brown-Forman, Inc., which in turn is owned by Jack Daniels.

Today, we may enjoy seeing some of the world's finest china here in New Jersey, something that Walter Scott Lenox was never able to do. Unfortunately, he went totally blind before his company created the fine china that made Tiffany's and President Wilson stand up and take notice.

Dr. T. C. Wheaton: From Clamdigger to Wealthy Industrialist

One of the greatest businessmen in South Jersey history has to be Dr. T. C. Wheaton of Millville, New Jersey. Trained as a pharmacist, he turned his attention to making the bottles in which pharmaceuticals were sold. Today, the company that bears his name employs nearly 3,000 people in Millville plus 7,000 more at factories in other areas.

Theodore Corson Wheaton was born in Tuckahoe on August 24, 1852, one of five sons of Amos and Harriet Wheaton. Like so many other South Jerseyans, he cut his teeth on oysters and made his first money clamming and oystering in local bays. As a teenager, he sailed for a year on a 400-ton coaster vessel.

But the waterman's life was not to be for T. C. Wheaton. Towards the end of his teenage years, Wheaton became apprenticed to a pharmacist in South Seaville—Dr. Way. In the late 1800s, pharmacy as a science was still in its infancy. There was no Food and Drug Administration, and hundreds of medical messiahs and "toadstool millionaires," as historians now call them, plied their elixirs all over the country. Wheaton rejected this type of pharmacy, choosing scientific training instead.

At the age of 21, he entered the Philadelphia College of Pharmacy and Science, graduating in 1876. From there, he went across the street and enrolled in the Medical College of the University of Pennsylvania. During his college years, Wheaton lived, slept, and ate pharmacy—figuratively speaking, that is. He boarded with a druggist, Frank Hayes, and worked in his shop. He received his M.D. degree in 1879. It was during this period that he met Bathsheba Brooks Lancaster of Philadelphia, and they were married in 1880.

The newlyweds set up housekeeping in South Seaville, but moved to Millville in 1882. In Millville, the Wheatons opened up a wallpaper and drug store on Broad Street, living over the store, as so many other proprietors did in those days. Apparently, if drug sales declined, they could sell wallpaper. Later, Wheaton sold this drug store, and bought and sold two others. These were Victorian drug stores, which frequently included ice cream parlors.

In Millville, Wheaton became friends with two other businessmen, William Shull and Eugene Goodwin, who operated a small glass factory nearby. When their firm got into trouble, Wheaton loaned them several thousand dollars. In 1888, he took over personal direction of the eight-pit furnace and gave up his medical practice. The rest is history: Wheaton grew into a worldwide corporation making glass and, later, plastics.

In those days, Millville turned out so much glass that Carl Sandburg was moved to write: "Down in southern New Jersey, they make glass. By day and by night, the fires burn on in Millville and bid the sand let in the light." What made it possible for a pharmacist to turn a small business into a financial empire? Perhaps it was the "education" he received clamming in the back bays. In clamming, everything depends on how hard you work.

Long before social responsibility became popular among businessmen, T. C. Wheaton was active in Millville's civic affairs. He was a member of the Board of Education from 1891 to 1896, and served on the city council from 1897 to 1913. In his spare time, he played his harmonica and told stories for his grandchildren. Dr. Wheaton died on September 30, 1931. Son Frank took over, and helped give the Wheaton company an international reputation.

Today, Wheaton Village in Millville stands as a reminder of the early days, when Wheaton Industries—and New Jersey—were in their infancy. It's worth a visit.

Richard Harris:
Pinelands Papermaking Baron

Richard Harris was the lord of Harrisville, a 19th century papermaking town in the Pines. If all the world is a stage (as Shakespeare put it) Harris was more than a bit player in South Jersey history. He was a leading man.

The town that is known today as Harrisville was founded by Isaac Potts, an ironmaster who built the Wading River Forge in 1795. It was located about 6 miles northwest of New Gretna in the Pine Barrens. The Forge passed through the hands of a number of men, including Samuel Read of Batsto, until William McCarty bought it in 1832. In a stroke of entrepreneurial genius, McCarty began shifting production from iron to paper. It was a decision that would provide jobs and create a beautiful South Jersey community for another generation. The days of South Jersey iron were past.

McCarty produced paper until 1851, when Richard Harris entered the scene. Along with his brother William, these two young mainline Philadelphians begged, borrowed, and earned the $6,000 needed to buy the sawmill, gristmill, mansion house, tenant houses, store, barns, and stables.

It is appropriate that this area should still be known as Harrisville, because Richard Harris was made to lead a company town. All the evidence suggests that Harris loved his town and its people, and they in turn loved him. A lifelong bachelor, the town would become his "lady," the inhabitants his "children."

Historian Angela N. Delloma describes Harris as "a man of unquestionable character, impeccable neatness, and sober independence." His grandniece described him as "a bachelor who never missed an opportunity to dance with a pretty lady."

In the autumn of 1856, Richard Harris moved into William McCarty's mansion, or more accurately, a large country farmhouse. To tend the mansion and add some feminine warmth, Harris hired an Irish maid, Mary McCoy. She could neither read or write, but was a light-hearted soul with a soft-pitched Irish brogue who darned his socks, cooked his meals, and otherwise added feminine charm to a womanless household.

109

Soon there were 75 people filling other village houses. There was also a boarding house, where unmarried men could pay for the privilege of home-cooked meals. A general store was well stocked so that company employees could buy what they needed. Eventually, Harris installed cast-iron gas street lamps. At Christmas, Harris gave each of his employees a plump Christmas turkey and each employee's child candies and nuts. The town's doorways and windows were decorated with pine boughs and holly and wreaths of laurel. Christmas trees were decorated with strings of popped corn and wild cranberries. To round out this piece of Victorian Americana, Harris sponsored a company baseball team that played teams from nearby Jenkin's Neck and other small towns.

Richard Harris also provided for community entertainment. Fairs and picnics were common. One mid-August festival in 1880 included performances by the Germania Coronet Band of Egg Harbor City. A public school was also set up to educate the children, as well as a church. Eventually, Richard's brother Howard came to live with him, livening up life in the mansion with his wife and children. One thing, however, that Richard Harris didn't provide for his people was alcohol. Harris felt that liquor would destroy the moral fiber of his Harrisville community.

The town, of course, existed to run the paper mill. The main product at Harrisville was a thick, heavy, brown paper known as butcher's paper. At one point, Harrisville was the most productive paper plant in the United States.

Manila rope was one of the main ingredients for making paper, along with old rags, scrap paper, bagging, and salt hay. These ingredients would be cut and melted down into a pulp, the moisture squeezed out, and then pressed into paper. The whole process was a secret known only to Richard Harris and a few confidants.

For a time, the mill was one of the largest in America. Water channeled and "raced" from the Wading River powered the mill, and often work went on around the clock.

Creating jobs and managing businesses through tough times requires aggressive management, and that was provided by Richard Harris. But when Harris grew old, Harrisville's fortunes began to wane. The property passed briefly through Joseph Wharton's hands, but even he could not revive it. Despite attempts to get the Raritan and Delaware Railroad (later the New Jersey Central) to build a line to Harrisville, the railroad was built 8 miles to the West, leading to the demise of papermaking at Harrisville. In 1914, a bad forest fire swept through and destroyed much of the town.

Today, there are but a few ruins, now owned by the state—a silent reminder of the days when Richard Harris reigned over a Victorian village deep in the Pines.

Dr. Charles Smith:
His Patients Took to the Waters

In the late 1800s, a German doctor named Charles Smith was taking a walk near Egg Harbor's Union Creek. Suffering from numerous aches and pains, Dr. Smith fell into the creek. Wading across the creek to the other side, Smith found that upon coming out of the water his pains were gone. Smith was convinced that the cedar waters had special healing effects. Wanting to share this discovery with others, Smith founded his health resort. Several buildings were constructed. Although today only the roundhouse, or sun house exists, along with Smith's man-made canals, back then patients flocked to Smith's health resort from New York and Philadelphia, making Egg Harbor part of the Atlantic City–Cape May resort system.

Dr. Smith's main treatment consisted of having his patients walk through canals against the current. As they walked through the canal, they would cross their arms and slap their hands on opposite shoulders. Smith told them to dip down in the cedar water so that their entire body could benefit from its healing effects. The patients would snack on bananas and dry rolls after they went through the treatment.

After the patient finished a prescribed number of laps, he would go across the street to a building that had a windmill on top. In this building were radiators that helped the patient dry out. Known as the Roundhouse, it now serves as Egg Harbor's Historical Museum.

If an individual had a problem area, such as a leg that ached, Smith would give him the hot mud treatment. Theoretically, the cedar water in the mud and the heat would have a salutary effect on the problem area.

Smith was also a strong believer in "proper" eating habits. He insisted that no one should drink anything during or immediately after a meal. Smith believed that liquids diluted the digestive juices, an idea that has since been verified by modern science. Coffee was forbidden. Instead, Smith had his patients drink a specially prepared tea and a special cocoa made from cocoa shells. For dessert, Smith usually served fruit. Prunes were especially popular. According to a former employee, prunes were purchased by the crate.

111

Medicine was also available at the health resort. The medicine was made from the herbs and roots in the nearby woods and were mixed together personally by Smith. The medicine was made in large vats located in Smith's office. Smith's medicine cost $1 a bottle. One lady said that it tasted terrible, but that it cured her cold.

Smith's health resort was incorporated in 1905, and was sold to Henry Wimberg in 1921. Smith passed away sometime between 1921 and 1926. His reputation outlasted him. Smith was considered by many in Egg Harbor to be eccentric. Certainly he "marched to the beat of a different drummer." He demanded that his prescriptions be followed to the letter. If someone refused, he would say, "Get out of my house!" He also claimed to have been born in 1776. And even in the early 1900s, his long white beard set him apart from his peers.

Egg Harbor City's Health Resort was advertised in North Jersey, Philadelphia, and other metropolitan areas on the East Coast. Today, if you live in the South Jersey area, you can take advantage of Dr. Smith's regimen without leaving home. Just take to the cedar waters, walk in the pines, breathe the air, and eat lots of prunes. Who knows, maybe you'll live to be 146, as Dr. Smith supposedly did.

Photo of Dr. Charles Smith is courtesy of The Egg Harbor City Historical Society in Egg Harbor.

SIMON LAKE: HE INVENTED THE SUBMARINE

When it was first written, *Jules Verne's 20,000 Leagues Under the Sea* and the underwater world it depicted seemed impossible. Yet one boy believed such a craft as the Nautilus could be built, a boy who grew up daydreaming along the beach in Ocean City. His name was Simon Lake.

Simon Lake was a grandson of the man by the same name who had mortgaged his Pleasantville farm to finance the development of a religious resort called Ocean City. During the course of his lifetime, the younger Lake invented, among other things, a machine for capping cans, prefabricated houses, an under-river tunnel system, and a successful submarine. Today, all countries that have submarines use Lake's patents.

One of Lake's first jobs was with his father's shade-roller manufacturing business, which was located on 10th and West in Ocean City. Here he learned the practical aspects of iron working and traveled to and from Philadelphia to learn mechanical drawing.

In 1893, the U.S. Navy advertised for designs for a submarine torpedo boat. Inspired by Jules Verne, Lake submitted plans for a vessel called the *Argonaut,* a design that included wheels on the bottom to enable it to ride on the ocean floor. It also had a diving compartment that would allow divers to leave the ship underwater.

Unfortunately for both Lake and the U.S. Navy, another design was accepted, that of Irish-American inventor John Holland. It was unfortunate for Lake, for his designs were just as good. Indeed, the idea of submerging by negative buoyancy, which he pioneered, is still in use today. And it was unfortunate for the U.S. Navy, for Holland had other plans for his submarine technology—plans that included using submarines in an Irish rebellion against England. Lake's first submarine, by contrast, was built for peaceful use—for exploration.

Holland's submarine, the *U.S.S. Holland,* was launched in 1898. It was the U.S. Navy's first submarine. Spurned by the U.S. government, Lake traveled around the world trying to interest other nations in his submarine. Lake eventually wound up a long way from Ocean City in St. Petersburg, Russia, where the old Russia under the czars bought his idea and began construction of submarines. During the Russia-Japanese War in 1905, the Lake submarine was one of the few successes the Russians experienced in their losing war against Japan.

When other governments, including Italy and Germany, tried to entice Lake away from Russia (where he worked under the alias of E. Simons) the Russians offered him 5 million rubles to stay.

Eventually, Lake returned to the United States and built his own shipyard at Bridgeport, Connecticut, where he realized his dream of building submarines for his native land. Holland's company, meanwhile, had gone belly-up, and Holland had died penniless in 1914.

When Lake died in 1945 he was not a rich man. While traveling through other countries, spies had stolen many of his patents. He did have one special reward, though: the praise and admiration of the man who had first inspired his vision, Jules Verne. Verne had telegraphed him and said of the ship: "Her conspicuous success will push on underwater navigation all over the world."

Lake eventually did receive belated recognition from the U.S. government, when the world's largest submarine tender was named the *U.S.S. Simon Lake* in 1964.

The moral of the story? Never discount the power of a great book, a South Jersey beach, and a child's imagination. Such is the stuff that dreams are made of.

ELIZABETH WHITE: SHE DEVELOPED THE FIRST CULTIVATED BLUEBERRIES

Today, New Jersey is one of the leading producers of blueberries in the world. Hammonton, in Atlantic County, claims to be the blueberry capital of the world. And when President Reagan visited the area in 1984, he was presented with (what else?) a blueberry pie.

But it wasn't always that way. Through much of our history, blueberries were known only to local people and were picked in the wild. Two varieties of blueberries grew naturally in the swamps and barrens of New Jersey—the highbush and the lowbush. Both thrive in the acidic soil that produces famous Jersey tomatoes and cranberries. Ironically, it was the cranberry that first gained wide acceptance, while the much sweeter blueberry was still left uncultivated. If there was time after work on the cranberry bogs, blueberries could be picked as an added bonus.

It took a determined woman—Elizabeth White of Whitesbog in Burlington County—to turn the blueberry from an afterthought into an institution. Born in 1872 at Whitesbog, deep in the Pine Barrens, she grew up on her father's cranberry farm. He was one of the first to harvest the berry systematically. Learning her father's trade well, she became the first female member of the American Cranberry Association. Highly respected by other cranberry growers, she eventually became the association's first female president.

In 1910, White read in an article that the U.S. Department of Agriculture was seriously interested in developing blueberries. By 1916, she had formed an informal partnership with Dr. Frederick V. Coville of the Department of Agriculture, and they attempted to cultivate blueberries in New Jersey. The nation's first commercial shipment of cultivated blueberries was made from Miss White's farm in 1916.

Financing much of the operation, White journeyed through the woods seeking bigger and better huckleberry plants. She also encouraged friends and neighbors to look for them, and named the best after their finders. In a 1953 interview, Miss White (she never married) said that the "keystone" of the cultivated

116

Artwork of Elizabeth White is courtesy of the Conservation and Environmental Center at Whitesbog.

blueberry was the Rubel, named for Rube Leek of Chatsworth. Others helped develop more varieties: the June, introduced in 1930; the Weymouth, introduced in 1936; the Berkeley and Coville, 1949; and the Bluecrop, 1952. But it was Elizabeth White's efforts that really put New Jersey on the map as a blueberry grower. Today, blueberries can be found all over the world—in pies, jams, muffins, danishes, and just by themselves.

As historian John T. Cunningham put it, "Elizabeth White never sought fame; instead fame found its way to her at Whitesbog." Someone once said that if you stay in one place long enough, the world will come to you. They should have added that you also have to be diligent in that one place.

In 1954, she died among the pines, blueberries, and cranberries that had surrounded her in life. Today, Miss White and the blueberry are an important part of our New Jersey heritage. Picking blueberries was one of my first jobs, and I learned a lot about life and hard work out in those fields. Hopefully, future New Jerseyans will have the same opportunity to partake of White's legacy.

117

VICTOR MOORE:
DOWN JERSEY'S MOST FAMOUS ACTOR

"All the world's a stage, and we're but players in it" might have been the watchword of Victor Moore, South Jersey's most famous native-born actor. By the end of his career, Victor Moore had become one of America's most beloved theatrical figures.

The actor was born in Hammonton in Atlantic county on February 2, 1876. His first antics took place in a house on Twelfth Street and on the floor of his father's grocery store on South Second Street. Moore's father, Orville E. Moore, was one of Hammonton's pioneers, having come to South Jersey from Vermont. Moore went to a one-room schoolhouse in Hammonton, learning about the great actors on the stage of history.

He received his first taste of stage life at the age of 10. A well-known 19th century touring troupe, the Guy Brothers Minstrels, had made a visit to Hammonton. A stagehand was needed, so Moore volunteered. Five years later, he graduated from working behind the scenes and was asked to perform with the Acme Dramatic Company of Hammonton, a little theater group organized by Dr. J. C. Waas. This was in Union Hall at Third Street and Vine. An old story says that young Moore was booed and hissed off the stage, and that he made a vow never to again perform in Hammonton. Apparently the Pineys who lived in Hammonton were not refined enough to appreciate his talents.

A year later, Moore's family moved to Boston. Here 16-year-old Victor made his professional debut in *Babes in the Woods*, which opened in Boston. His pay was only 4 dollars per week. But he had been hired by John Drew, father of the famous Barrymore clan, and worked with Ethel Barrymore. What his family thought of his entrance into theatrical life is not known, although the general opinion in his day was that it was not a good choice for a career. It provided only an unstable form of income, working often away from the restraints and stability of family.

By 1894, Moore could be counted among the few really successful actors in America, touring the country and making his mark in theatrical history. Among his many stage successes were *Of Thee I Sing, Louisiana Purchase, Let 'Em Eat Cake, Everything Goes,* and *Leave It to Me.* Hollywood coaxed him away from Broadway, where he performed in *Romance in the Rain, Gold Diggers of 1937,* and a film version of *Louisiana Purchase.*

Moore loved the stage so much that he continued handling big parts into his 80s. He was the George Burns of the mid-20th century. His last stage appearance was in the New York City Center's revival of the musical *Carousel.* His last contribution to the motion pictures was as a bungling plumber in *The Seven Year Itch.* Critics say he stole the show. By this time he had also become famous for his portrayal of the imaginary Vice President Throttlebottom, a satirical presentation of the role of an American vice president. Moore's fame attracted a number of people who wanted to give him financial advice, but none of the investments worked out.

Victor Moore died on July 23, 1962, at the age of 86. And what of his vow to never act again in Hammonton? He couldn't help but break it, as his movies could be seen in moviehouses and eventually on every Hammonton television set.

The Diary of Isabella Peterson Leek

Her name was Isabella Peterson Leek, and she lived at the turn of the 20th century. She was not a suffragette, a temperance leader, or a pioneer woman, aviator, entrepreneur, or athlete. What makes her important to American history is that, in spite of a hectic schedule supporting her husband, feeding and clothing her family, burying her loved ones, and ringing the neck of an occasional chicken for dinner, she found time to keep a diary. Written before airplanes, before automobiles, and before rural electrification, her diary gives us a glimpse of the difficult times faced by our ancestors just a couple of generations ago.

The year was 1900, but it might as well have been 1700 in the Batsto, Pleasant Mills, Nesco, and Pinelands areas. Except for the railroad, life in the Pines of New Jersey had changed little in 200 years. Living on the edge of a wilderness (now the Pinelands National Preserve) and with few conveniences, her life is representative of the millions of women who worked behind he scenes to build the region and nation. Our grandmothers and great-grandmothers were made of stern stuff.

Born Isabella Elizabeth Peterson, she was the daughter of Isaac and Elizabeth (Southard) Peterson. Among her brothers and sisters were Jennie May, who married Charles Green, author of a popular history of the Batsto and Pleasant Mills areas, and my grandfather, Clarence Junius Peterson. On December 23, 1893, she married George Leek of Wading River, and set up housekeeping at Pleasant Mills, where George ran the mill.

At first glance, her diary is a record of the agricultural year to which most of our forefathers were subject. In January of 1900, she records that the "Mill was shut down because of frozen water." In February, the snow was so deep that church had to be cancelled. By April 14, the spring thaw had set in, as she "Planted poppy seeds today." On the 21st, like so many other Piney's, she went "searching for trailing arbutus today." She found the first ripe huckleberries on June 16. These were the days before cultivated blueberries; only people who picked them wild in South Jersey or Maine could enjoy them. On July 20 she reported that "Fruit and vegetables were all drying up for want of rain." The produce made it, however, for on August 20 her entry reads: "Have been busy canning peaches." On September 17 and 18 the first heavy frost came that year, and she recorded that the cranberries were nearly gone.

The big event that year, however, was the birth of her baby girl on October 19. Named Helen Gertrude Leek, Isa recorded that "She weighs twelve lbs, has lots of black hair, and everyone says they never saw such a fat baby!" For 1900, that was indeed a good birthweight. That Thanksgiving, they had a duck for the main course. In those days, people ate what was available or in season; and the custom of everyone eating turkey on Thanksgiving was not yet fully established.

Death was a constant companion of our forebears, in the days before inoculation and miracle drugs like aspirin and penicillin. For the year 1901 she records such details as "Harold Doughty died today of croup and pneumonia. Only taken sick a day before, age 13 years. . . Nancy Wescoat's little boy, Harold, died today of congestion of the lungs, aged 2 and a half years. . . Will Johnson buried another child today, eight months old."

In addition to sickness and death, Pinelands' dwellers also faced the constant danger of forest fire. In forests composed of bull-pine trees, fire is a natural and necessary phenomena, for fire is the only thing hot enough to open the pinecones and release the seeds. The tower on the Batsto mansion was built to keep a lookout for fire. Some fires were started in homes or barns, such as was the case on April 27, 1900. Isa wrote: "Terrible fire at Pleasant Mills, commenced a few minutes after eleven o'clock. Started by John Reynolds' barn, destroyed all the out buildings. Went from there to Catholic Church, destroyed that. Frank Mathis' house and hay barn, Patrick Love's house, Mrs. Henricke's and Mr. Wilson's house and the Mechanic's Hall all destroyed in a few hours. Very little was saved from any of the houses." The next day, she wrote that the fires were still burning. These words have been said many times in South Jersey history, as fire has always been a constant threat. Fortunately, each little community eventually established its own volunteer fire company of dedicated individuals, whose growing expertise and training have helped to make the Pine Barrens a safer place in which to live.

Dark clouds hung over September of 1901, as Isa recorded faraway events that nevertheless had implications for all Americans. For the 6th she wrote, "President McKinley shot at the Pan American Exposition at Buffalo;" on the 13th she wrote the sad news, "President McKinley died today at 2 A.M." Isa apparently knew that she was part of a greater world than the Pine Barrens. Other entries concerning national events include floods in the West and presidential elections. There are no entries about international affairs; before World War I, America was still in the Age of Innocence, as historian Henry May put it.

On Christmas Eve, 1901, Isabella had an accident that was to cost her an eye. By January 4, she wrote: "My eye seems to be doing nicely. Have not had much soreness." By February 27, she went to town (Philadelphia, by rail) and had a glass eye put in. In those days, you could have a glass eye inserted for 4 dollars. However, if she wanted to dwell on her misfortune, there was little time. In February, she wrote: "Smallpox in Hammonton." Today, we have no idea how pervasive was the fear brought on by a smallpox epidemic. Isa would have been especially concerned about her daughter. Providentially, smallpox didn't reach Pleasant Mills, and today, modern medicine has pretty much wiped out smallpox in the Western world.

Life was not all hardship and hard work. Because there was no TV or easy transportation by way of automobiles, people had to make their own local entertainment and fellowship. It is surprising, for example, to see how much was going on in Nesco, a little agricultural community outside of Hammonton. The diary mentions "Sociable at Nesco," "Festival at Nesco," and "Lawn Party at Nesco," several times. Little Nesco was a partying town! On July 21, Isa attended a festival at Herman City. Today, Herman City is an overgrown ghost town along the Mullica River.

Church attendance and fellowship was also important. The diary records Isa's attendance at church, revival meetings, even trips to Pitman Grove, which was still echoing with the sermons of the famous South Jersey preacher, Charlie Pitman. In Isa's day, her brother, William Lawrence Peterson, was a Methodist minister who lived in Pitman and published *The Pitman Grove Messenger.*

Above all else, the diary contained reference to her family. On March 25, she mentions going to Philadelphia with her brother (my grandfather) Clarence: "Clarence and I went to the city. He had his teeth pulled and I had my eye changed." Then there are, of course, references to her daughter, Helen—when new teeth came in, how much she weighed on her birthday, and so on. On November 19, she put Helen in a colored dress. Up to about 2 years old, our forefathers dressed babies in white smocks. Putting a toddler in colored dresses was a milestone. It also meant that in those days of still fairly high infant mortality, the baby would probably live.

The year 1902 ends with this entry for Christmas: "Christmas tree put up on Christmas Eve, and stayed up through Epiphany." In the early 1900s, this was the custom, unlike today when Christmas trees generally go up much earlier. The diary goes on in like fashion until 1906, when she presumably became too busy to continue.

Isabella "Isa" Peterson Leek, born in Pleasant Mills on January 13, 1871, died on December 28, 1953, at the home of her second daughter, Laura Hudson, in Wilmington, Delaware. She was buried in the Pleasant Mills cemetery, one of the oldest in the region. Because of diaries like Isa's, we have a better glimpse of life in the past and the kind of women who worked behind the scenes to nurture our families and build the nation. So write in your own diary today—you could become a part of our American heritage.

Eldridge R. Johnson:
He Perfected the Victrola

Camden, New Jersey, South Jersey's biggest city, has a storied past. Years ago, people took so much pride in their city houses that each resident kept the area in front of his dwelling perfectly clean. Camden was the home of Walt Whitman, the Campbell's Soup kids, and the famous New York Shipbuilding Company. But it was also the home of the Victor Talking Machine Company, founded in 1894 by Eldridge R. Johnson, who became the mass-producer of the famous RCA-Victor Victrola.

According to legend, a young lady by the name of Ada Crossley walked into the studio of the new Victor Talking Machine Company in Camden on April 30, 1903, and sang "Cara Mio Ben." She then put on her coat and hat and walked out of the studio, having made the first Victor Red Seal Record. Millions of recordings would follow. In actuality, Miss Crossley recorded three songs—not in Camden, but in New York—and they weren't the first.

Even though Thomas Edison invented the talking machine in Menlo Park, New Jersey, in 1877, it remained for Eldridge Johnson of Camden to improve upon it. In 1894 he was 27 years old and a machinist and partner in the industrial firm of Scull and Johnson. Ambitious and energetic, he bought Scull's interest as well as his contract with Emil Berliner, who had invented the flat disc record. By 1901, he had formed the Victor Talking Machine Company. The name Victor came from a popular bicycle that was being sold in Camden at the turn of the century.

People who have never seen a real Victrola up close still know what one looks like from the famous "His Master's Voice" painting, which became the trademark for RCA-Victor. As America's growing middle class began to be able to afford such an instrument in their homes, Johnson brought some of the greatest names in music to Camden including Enrico Caruso, Melba, Fritz Kreisler, Rachmaninoff, McCormack, Scotti, Martinelli, and Galli-Curci. Caruso's royalties were 50 cents a record, very high for the time. But Johnson was trying to build market share with a new product, and it was a good investment. To introduce its red seal records, the Victor Company maintained a concert hall on the Atlantic City

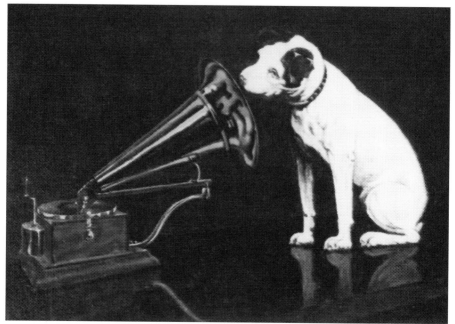

*Francis Barraud's "His Master's Voice" painting, depicting the RCA dog
and the Victrola, was created by Eldridge R. Johnson.*

boardwalk. And so, for a brief moment in time, not New York, not Vienna or
Rome, but Camden and Atlantic City had become the musical capitals of the
world. RCA-Victor's trademark picture, which became just as famous as the Victrola itself, was based on London artist Francis Barraud's 1890 painting. Barraud
had painted his fox terrier Nipper with his head cocked, listening to a gramophone. Barraud titled it "His Master's Voice" and tried to sell it, but the art houses
and dealers turned it down as being unreal. Finally, Gramophone, Ltd., of England bought the painting and used it as an advertisement. So impressed was Johnson with the picture that he bought the Western Hemisphere rights, leaving
Gramophone the European rights to the picture. Today, Nipper is one of the most
famous dogs painted, although most people don't even know his name. "His
Master's Voice" consequently appeared on thousands of RCA-Victor products.

Eldridge Johnson eventually settled in historic Moorestown, New Jersey, where
he died on November 14, 1945, but not before leaving a great deal to philan-
thropy. He endowed the Community House and Episcopal Church in
Moorestown, the Johnson Foundation in Medical Physics at the University of
Pennsylvania, the Cooper Branch of the Free Library of Camden, and the Community Church at Dover, Delaware, where he was raised. RCA has since been
broken into smaller divisions, many of which have been bought and sold several times in corporate takeovers.

Henry Hettinger:
South Jersey's Pioneer Aviator

When people think of New Jersey's inventive genius, Thomas Edison's Menlo Park comes to mind, as does Bell Labs and other great research centers. One New Jersey inventor who is often overlooked is Henry Hettinger of Bridgeton. At the same time the Wright brothers were experimenting with their first planes, Hettinger was designing and building an airplane here in New Jersey. He did not beat the Wright brothers to the punch, but was so close behind them he might have been their shadow.

Hettinger's ancestors were from Switzerland, land of goat-herders and precision clock- and toolmakers. Both his father and mother worked in the famous Krupp Iron Works in Baden-Baden, Germany, before emigrating to Stroudsburg, Pennsylvania. When young Henry was a year and a half old, they moved to Bridgeton.

In those days, Bridgeton was an official Federal Port of Entry and was known for welcoming talented immigrants and other outsiders. Hettinger showed an aptitude for mechanical work at an early age. In 1891, at the age of 16, he built a working steam engine measuring about a foot long that was later used in local schools for science demonstrations. Not long after, he went to work for another inventor, Oberlin Smith, who is credited with the concept of magnetic recording and breakthroughs in metallurgy.

In 1898, he opened the Hettinger Engine Company on Broad Street. In starting this business, Hettinger was much like the early pioneers in the computer industry, only the new technology he was working with was gasoline engines. Hettinger's business soon prospered, with many engines being sold to the oyster industry to power shipboard winches. To both diversify his business and pursue his own interests, he began working on an airplane engine in 1908.

By 1910, Hettinger had developed a biplane having a 40 horsepower, six-cylinder engine, and an aluminum and wood frame. His wife, Mary, sewed the fabric wings. Built under a large tent on Grove Street, Hettinger tested the plane on the west side of the Cohansey River, where farmers harvested salt hay. In the first tests, Hettinger taxied the plane back and forth, but didn't lift off.

On September 19, 1910, Hettinger tried to fly his plane at the Cumberland County Fairgrounds. Rising 12 feet into the air, the plane pitched and came crashing down. Spectators screamed, thinking Hettinger was dead. Fortunately, Hettinger was able to crawl out and had no injuries.

Undaunted, Hettinger returned to the drawing board. Less than a month later, on October 15, he was ready. It was on that day he had his first successful flight, lifting into the air six times. This was perhaps the first successful flight in New Jersey history.

Hettinger went on to design a seaplane, but stopped making engines for planes after 1915. His daughter, Bertha Coombs, says her father never really trusted his engine and didn't want to see anyone get hurt.

He served on the Board of Education, and City Council and the Red Cross during World War I, and he was an officer at the Farmers and Merchants Bank. He also owned two oyster schooners. He died in 1931, at the relatively young age of 56. His wife, Mary, who had sewn the wings on his plane, lived long enough to see a man walk on the moon. She was among the few who knew that it was her husband, Henry Hettinger, who had taken the first baby steps to make that "giant leap for mankind" possible.

CHARLES F. SEABROOK:
NEW JERSEY'S GREATEST 'TRUCK' FARMER

South Jersey has traditionally been known for its truck farms, and perhaps the greatest truck farmer of them all was Charles F. Seabrook of Cumberland County. At its height in the 1950s and '60s, Seabrook Farms was the largest farm-freezing operation in the world.

The word "truck" as related to farming comes from the French, and means "to barter or peddle." Early truck farmers in South Jersey would grow a variety of vegetables, then peddle them in nearby towns.

In the 1800s, Arthur Seabrook had a 57-acre truck farm in Cumberland County. Over the years, his small farm gained a reputation for producing vegetables of superior quality. By 1900, he was shipping premium quality fresh vegetables to markets patronized by the wealthy in Philadelphia, New York, and Baltimore. Rejecting all but the most perfect fruits and vegetables, Seabrook shipped the fruits of his labor in barrels by rail.

It remained for Arthur's son, Charles Franklin Seabrook, to turn Seabrook farms into an international operation. Charles, or C. F., showed his flair for scientific agriculture even as a young man. When he was 14, he learned of a farmer in Denmark who had strung perforated iron pipes over a field to create artificial rain in times of drought. Seabrook tried the experiment on a celery bed, and was so successful that Seabrook Farms soon had the largest overhead irrigation system in the world. It was estimated that such irrigation increased crop returns by 200-300 percent.

By 1917, Charles had built his agriculture empire into a farm of over 3,000 acres. He was described by those who knew him as "a man with the green thumb of a Burbank and the business acumen of a Rockefeller." In the first copy of the company newspaper, C. F. Seabrook declared, "I'm proud of the fact that I'm a farmer. Don't know of another trade in the world I'd swap for!"

In 1922, Seabrook added a cannery to his holdings. Ten years later, he produced his first frozen vegetables. Seabrook then invited Clarence Birdseye of New York down to cooperate in selling frozen vegetables. Birdseye had hit upon his own methods while in Canada studying the eating habits of the Eskimos. Today, thanks partly to Seabrook, Birdseye is a household word.

Long before the recent move back to organic gardening, Seabrook was practicing good ecology. All natural organic waste was plowed back into the soil to build it up.

In the late 1920s, Seabrook experienced financial difficulties that forced him to temporarily transfer ownership of Seabrook Farms to Del Bay Farms. Later, in 1929—not the best year to begin a new investment—Seabrook, with a group of investors, bought his company back.

The 1930s were tough times for Seabrook, as they were for just about everyone else. But as Charles' sons, Belford, Jack, and John, moved into the business, and World War II increased the demand for packaged food, Seabrook Farms eventually became the food processing industry's wonder of the world. Soon businesses were coming from all over the world to view Seabrook's Upper Deerfield Township operations. The unique thing about Seabrook Farms was that, to a great extent, Seabrook had shown that agriculture could be industrialized. Seabrook Farms was considered to be such a model of efficiency that *Time* magazine did a feature story on the enterprise.

As an employer, Charles Seabrook was from the old school. He was extremely loyal to those who came in early and cleaned up after their jobs were done, but had little time for those who did not work hard. Casper Gasperini, in an interview with the *Philadelphia Inquirer* several years ago, said of the Seabrooks: "You didn't get rich working here, but the Seabrooks were good people. They treated people right, gave everyone respect. No one was ever looked down upon."

Seabrook required little sleep, and was happiest during the times of year when crops were being harvested and processed around the clock. Workers tell of how he would visit someone on the packing line at 3:00 a.m. and suggest how the work could be done better.

The saddest chapter in Seabrook history came in 1959, when C. F. was 78 years old. In the beginning of that year, he refused to renew a voting trust required by the banks that financed the operation and who were in favor of granting control of the company to his son Jack. According to F. Alan Palmer's history of Upper Deerfield Township, *This Place Called Home*, Charles refused to accept the fact that he was old and ill and that his three sons were ready to assume control. C. F. could have slowly released his grip on the company and become the "elder statesman" of the food processing industry. Instead, he planned to control every aspect of the company until he took his last breath. In an effort to save the company, his wife and children filed suit to have Mr. Seabrook declared mentally incompetent. They lost, and Seabrook sold the food processing plant to Seeman Brothers. Over the next 23 years, the rest of the lands and assets were sold off. In 1982, the last 97 workers were dismissed by a subsidiary. At one time, however, Seabrook Farms was one of the world leaders in food processing.

Miss Antoinette Doell:
'America Was Schoolmistresses'

South Jersey has had no lack of strong women who helped shape our history. One can think of Elizabeth Haddon, who founded Haddonfield, or Cornelia Hancock, who helped found the modern nursing profession. Others made their mark teaching the rising generation. One such woman, who taught English and morals for over 50 years, was Miss Antoinette Doell, or "our Miss Nettie" as the townspeople called her in her native Egg Harbor City.

Born in Galloway Township on January 26, 1876, the daughter of Philip and Emilie Doell, Antoinette Doell was educated in Egg Harbor City schools. After graduation, she attended Keystone State Normal School in Pennsylvania. Returning to Egg Harbor in 1894, she started as a second grade teacher and devoted herself to one town, and one school system, for the next half-century. Today, such dedication is rare. But for a woman like Miss Doell, it was as natural as breathing.

Such longevity, coupled with a strong work ethic, gave Miss Doell special power and influence. From 1933 to 1941, for example, she wrote a column for the *Egg Harbor News* on school news and the activities of the local children. She used the opportunity to highlight the students' achievements and keep educational issues and activities in the public eye. She would comment on everything from athletic news to the latest debate team victory or spelling bee. One column began, "I am sorry to announce that this year there will be no County story-telling contest." Some readers and students no doubt breathed a sigh of relief—who needs a story-telling contest anyway? But for Nettie Doell, she really was sorry for this missed educational and cultural opportunity. The educational column was a "bully pulpit." In March of 1934, in the depths of the Depression, she announced that report cards were being sent home and that some students needed to take heed lest they fail for the year. "Not all children are gifted alike," she wrote. "Some can build a chicken coop while others can work out difficult Algebra problems. But the children who worry us most are those that could do better. They trifle away their time, in school and out, year after year, and when time for promotion comes, they are a dreadful disappointment to themselves and their parents."

She didn't mince words to students, either. Ron Hesse remembers, "Sure, I spent a lot of time in her office, to get me to shape up." She said, "Why don't you quit school if you don't like it here?" Ron did shape up, and became one of the founders of the new Egg Harbor Historical Museum. Because of intangible influences like hers, Ron and many others have a deep and abiding respect for local history and culture. Betty Morgenweck remembers that even in her last years of supervising, Miss Doell "though small and grandmotherly, still had a mailed fist in a velvet glove. You knew she must be obeyed."

Yet she also had a wry sense of humor. When she retired, for example, she said, "It is nice to receive bouquets, especially before you are dead." She also said: "After 52 years, teaching sort of gets in your blood and so I really do not feel happy about giving it up. It does not seem long, since I only had to teach one year at a time!"

In 1944, while World War II was still raging, she was given a testimonial dinner at Egg Harbor City's American Hotel honoring her 50 years of teaching. Letters poured in literally from all over the world, since many of her former students were then fighting Hitler and Tojo. Yet her lessons and those of other teachers like her held these men in good stead. From somewhere at sea, a young sailor wrote, "You have always been a friend to all, ever willing and always ready to offer a hand." A few months later, this young man was killed in a naval battle.

School administrator David Rohrbach, speaking at the retirement dinner, said:

> I would place her human touch with the pupils above the subject matter she taught (English, History, and Debate). She insisted on good work from her pupils and got it, because she knew and they knew what was desired in a recitation. Her classroom work manifested itself in our competition with other schools. On several occasions in our debating over a period of eleven years, when we won 80% of the debates, I was asked: "Who is your teacher in Public Speaking?" I said: "Whatever merits there are is from Miss Doell's classroom teaching in English."

Pastor Clarence Roberts of Emmanuel Congregational Church praised her in this way:

> For more than thirty years I have known you, and observed your deep interest in each class of boys and girls during that time. You have gently touched your pupils' lives in many other ways, enlarging their wisdom, and equipping them to face life as loyal, patriotic citizens. I am confident that your years of faithful service are deeply appreciated by everyone, but especially by those who have been scattered around the world, where the very mention of Miss Nettie would instantly brighten faces with a radiant glow.

Retiring in 1946 after almost 53 years of teaching, she had trained the "Great Generation" that weathered the Depression and won World War II. If "America

Photo of Antoinette Doell is courtesy of The Egg Harbor Historical Society in Egg Harbor.

was Schoolmasters" as the poet Robert Coffin put it, it was also schoolmistresses, like Miss Antoinette Doell. After her retirement, she concentrated on writing a comprehensive history of Egg Harbor, that unique German-American city. The history appeared in serial form in the local paper, then later in full in *Egg Harbor's Centennial Book*. That year, 1955, Miss Doell was named Citizen of the Year. It was in this book, published the year before I was born, that I got my first taste of local history. Her insights are invaluable and cannot be found anywhere else. Thus, though I never had the privilege of meeting Miss Doell, she was, in a sense, my teacher, too—my Miss Nettie.

Sara Spencer Washington Built a South Jersey, National Business Empire

Two generations ago, it was difficult for women to succeed in business. It was even more difficult if you were African-American. That is what makes the story of South Jersey's Sara Washington so amazing: She overcame both of these obstacles and became one of America's most well-known entrepreneurs.

Born in Norfolk, Virginia, on June 6, 1889, the daughter of Joshua and Ellen Phillips, Sara Washington graduated from Norfolk Mission College and took further studies at Columbia University. In 1916, she came to Atlantic City—Jonathan Pitney's "El Dorado"—to seek her fortune. In the days before the Civil Rights Movement, she began to create an alternate system of businesses, charities, and recreational opportunities. First, she founded a small hairdressing shop in the northside. Like any entrepreneur worth his or her salt, she began to experiment with new and different cosmetic ideas. Years later, one of her experiments resulted in a patent for a new system of removing excessive curl in hair. In 1919, she founded Apex News and Hair Company. In time she maintained a laboratory and offices in Atlantic City (1801-1803 Arctic Avenue) and an office in New York City. In those days, many blacks were moving north looking for jobs in the Atlantic City hotels, creating a growing market for her services and products.

By day, she worked in her beauty salon. By night, she canvassed the city, selling cosmetic products. Eventually, her business empire included *Apex News Services* (a magazine for Apex beauticians and agents), Apex Laboratories, Apex Beauty School, and Apex Rest, an exclusive furnished rooming house for blacks. Among the locations where she operated beauty schools were Atlantic City, New York City, Washington, DC, Baltimore, Richmond, Chicago, Philadelphia, and Atlanta. Because of her efforts, Washington was able to create jobs for over 45,000 Apex agents, 215 chemists, and scores of laboratory technicians, office workers, teachers, and sales representatives. (Over 75 products were manufactured in her Atlantic City plant.)

Fearing that the owners might not want to sell to a black, or that the neighbors might try to block the deal, she was able to buy the Brigantine Hotel us-

133

ing straw parties. This was uncovered by local historian Jo Kapus, who combed the county records for information on the remarkable Sara Washington. Kapus found that at one point, the property was sold to a group of investors named Mr. Truth Eternal, Mrs. Peaceful Samuel, Meek and Lowly Joseph, Seraphim Light, etc. These individuals were none other than Sara Spencer Washington, who also evidently had a sense of humor.

Washington knew that life was more than just business—there was also church, family, and community life. So, just as she had set up an alternative system of businesses, she also began creating her own system of recreational activities and charities. In 1946, for example, indignant that blacks in the Atlantic City Easter Parade were not acknowledged—she started her own parade on Arctic Avenue. Referred to as the Northside Easter Parade, Washington was able to attract top judges year after year. The parade came to an end when Atlantic City was integrated in 1960.

Washington also bought and then operated the Apex Golf Course in Galloway Township, located right in the middle of prime German-American farm country. It was an unusual combination—but here African-American sportsmen and German-American farmers co-existed in peace, each minding his own business. Such cooperation often gets little attention in the media, but it is as much a part of our heritage as slavery, segregation, and other negative influences.

A self-made millionaire when a million dollars was a lot of money, she gave much of it back to local charities. During the Depression, she hired an open-cockpit plane to fly over Atlantic City and drop coupons for a quarter ton of coal. She contributed to local organizations of all races and creeds. She also donated properties for homes for wayward girls and for a summer camp.

Outside the public arena, she had a private life as well. During World War I, she was married to Isaac Washington, but the couple separated in 1919. In the mid-30s, Washington adopted a 7-year-old cousin who needed a guardian, Joan Cross. In 1944, she announced her marriage to Shumpert Logan, who later became secretary of the company.

Washington's only foray into politics was in 1938, when she was elected to the Republican County Committee. Locally, at least, the party of Lincoln was fulfilling its promise of political freedom for all. But it wasn't in politics that she made her impact; it was in her work ethic, entrepreneurial skills, and service to others. These activities in themselves were a greater political statement than running for office, since economic success and free markets form the basis for political freedom. Without a solid foundation in economics, constitutions and bills of rights are but empty promises. By showing that blacks could be just as successful or even more successful than whites, she paved the way for the civil rights legislation of the 1960s. In 1939, she was honored at the New York World's Fair as one of the world's 10 most distinguished businesswomen. She died in 1953, leaving a legacy of achievement and service.

Thomas O. Chisholm:
He Sang South Jersey's Praises

One of the greatest hymn writers of all time made his home in the midst of South Jersey's pines and farmlands. His name was Thomas O. Chisholm. The author of over 1,200 poems and hymns, Chisholm spent most of his adult life in Vineland, New Jersey.

Born on July 29, 1866, Chisholm lived nearly a century. Originally, he wasn't from South Jersey; he was raised in Simpson County, Kentucky, and he grew up working on a farm. At the age of 16, without any high school or other advanced training, he began teaching school in the same country schoolhouse where he had received his own education.

But the schoolroom proved too small a forum for his ideas. In 1887, he became associate editor of a small weekly newspaper. While in Franklin, he became a born-again Christian under the preaching of Dr. H. C. Morrison, a well-known evangelist.

Not long after, Chisholm left the secular press to become office editor of *The Pentecostal Herald* in Louisville, Kentucky. Chisholm married in 1903, pastored a church for a year, but then finally became a life insurance agent for Prudential. For the rest of his life, Chisholm would use his business to subsidize his writing—for writing never really brought him much money.

Chisholm moved to Vineland, New Jersey, in 1916 where he became a prominent Methodist layman. From his home on West Avenue, hundreds of poems and hymns were produced. The most well-known were "Great Is Thy Faithfulness" and "Living for Jesus."

Paul Hunsberger, one of South Jersey's best-known radio commentators (he is the host of "Off the Cuff" on WSNJ-Bridgeton, New Jersey's oldest FM station), remembers Chisholm well. Both were active in the Gideons, the organization that places Bibles in hotels and other public places. At a Gideons' convention held in Vineland, Hunsberger sang one of Chisholm's songs, "The Prodigal Son," as a solo. After he finished singing, Chisholm came up to Hunsberger and said, "I have never heard it sung with as much meaning as you just did." "Maybe that's because I was a prodigal son," Hunsberger later reflected. According to Hunsberger, Chisholm said that he often almost regretted writing one of his most popular hymns, "Living for Jesus," because of the shallowness with which most people sing it.

One of Chisholm's most timely poems is "Alone," which is about the spouse that is left behind when the other dies. The poem was left unfinished, waiting until one or the other passed away. When Mrs. Chisholm passed away on April 6, 1954, Chisholm finished the poem and added this note: "The closing stanza was written after the death of my beloved wife and is offered as the testimony of the survivor, he who stayed, the other gone, for the sorrowing who may read the poem, to the glorious adequacy of God's grace in time of bereavement." The poem was originally published in the *Vineland Times Journal*. Chisholm wrote at least two Christmas carols, "Emmanuel" and "Had There Been No Christmas Story," as well.

In 1956, Glen Bintz of Glendale Printing, a friend of Chisholm, printed a limited edition of Chisholm poems and hymns in a book called *Great Is Thy Faithfulness*.

Chisholm retired to the Methodist Home in Ocean Grove, New Jersey, and died not long afterward.

Patriots, pirates, and pineys, and yes, even poets—our New Jersey heritage includes them all.

Edmund Einsiedel:
German-American Artisan

In the days before mass production, automated factories, and throwaway goods, most things were handcrafted. Because it took longer to make a given product, there were less finished goods, and people took care of what they had. It was the age of the artisan.

Typical of the people of that era who built South Jersey and the nation was Edmund Einsiedel, master potter. Einsiedel lived in what was once the German-American town of Egg Harbor City in Atlantic County. For nearly half a century, pottery made or sold at Einsiedel's Egg Harbor Pottery was a staple in homes throughout Atlantic County. Today, pieces that survive are treasured family possessions, passed down from one generation to the next.

When Egg Harbor City was founded in 1854-55, the town's founders envisioned a town of hard-working German immigrants devoted to craftsmanship, small business, and scientific agriculture. Edmund's father, Julius, arrived in 1875 to help bring this vision to reality by founding a potter's shop. It is interesting to read the elder Einsiedel's naturalization papers, for in them, he renounces all allegiance to the King of Saxony, and pledges his fealty to the still young United States of America. Citizenship was important in those days, as were promises and covenants. In those days, a man's word was his bond.

Establishing a pottery business was hard work, but not impossible for an industrious young man. After a time of apprenticeship (usually 7 years, taken from the number of years the Biblical Jacob served Laban), a man could set up an existing barn or room in his house as a pottery. The only essential pieces of equipment would be a turning or throwing wheel, a mill for preparing the clay, and a kiln for firing the clay. Thus the cost of setting up a shop was small. It had to be, for in those days of heavy immigration our forefathers had plenty of muscle and ambition, but little else. Fortunately, clay was an abundant natural resource in and around Egg Harbor. An early Egg Harbor promotional piece reads, "Clay of an excellent quality for the production of pottery and bricks is found in large quantities here," and the industry was carried on here on a small scale for a number of years by Julius Einsiedel.

Growing up in a family business, young Edmund was never far from hard work. Like so many other children growing up in the late 19th century, he received "a liberal education in the way of chores," as the old *McGuffey Readers* put it. Egg Harbor City schools still gave half of their instruction in German, insuring that young people like Edmund would not forget their Teutonic origins, even if they were living in the Pine Barrens of New Jersey. His education was rounded out by 2 years as an apprentice to Wingender Brothers in Haddonfield, where he learned how to make stoneware. In the days of master craftsmanship and apprenticeships, the philosophy was that a nonfamily member could not only teach you new skills, but also give you a taste of the real business world. If your only work experience was in a family business, your parents may have unintentionally sheltered you or overlooked certain faults.

In 1924, Julius died, leaving the pottery to Edmund. In Edmund's day, the pottery had considerable appeal to local children, as they were fascinated by the various stages involved in the making of earthenware. Such steps included preparing the clay, "throwing" it on the wheel, and turning it into something useful; time was spent on the drying table, applying glaze, stacking pieces in the kiln, and during the cooling off process. In the days before television and occupational safety rules, going down to Mr. Einsiedel's pottery shop was an exciting thing to do!

An invoice dated August 7, 1937, indicates some of the things that were sold by Edmund Einsiedel—clayware, sewer pipes, flue linings, flower pots, vases, artware, kitchen containers and bowls, and stoneware. Today, many homes throughout the South Jersey area have pottery that was produced by the Einsiedels. Some are clearly identified with the phrase, Egg Harbor Pottery.

Many local teenagers found employment at the Egg Harbor Pottery. Resident Tom Walczak recalled, "Mr. Einsiedel would take you by the hand and lead you from one job to the next."

The business was carried on until 1958, when fire destroyed part of the operation. Edmund Einsiedel was 83 at the time, so it was decided not to rebuild. Einsiedel died in 1966 at the age of 91. The business had lasted nearly 80 years—not bad, when today we know that two out of three new businesses will fail within a year.

Einsiedel, in German, is related to the word, "loner," or hermit. But Einsiedel was no loner. He loved people, and was a family man. He would put on fireworks displays for the neighborhood children each Fourth of July, and regale his grandchildren with stories of the Great Blizzard of 1888 and old German Egg Harbor. One of his granddaughters, Nancy Henschel Peterson, remembers how he would take her to Philadelphia on business trips by train. He also sang in the regionally famous German male chorus, the Aurora Singers.

As his great-grandson, I knew him for several years before he died. He was my connection to the past, one who stimulated my interest in the history and

Photo of Edmund and Emma Einsiedel is courtesy of Nancy Henschel Peterson.

the values of the past. Hopefully, more people will realize the value of spending time with their families as Ed Einsiedel did. Their memories—and the values they represent—are essential not just for the quality of our lives, but for civilization's very survival.

HENRY ROWAN: SOUTH JERSEY MAN MADE U.S. PHILANTHROPIC HISTORY

In the spring of 1992, South Jersey industrialist Henry Rowan made history by pledging $100 million to Glassboro State College. It was the largest gift to a public college in the history of higher education. Not only did it infuse new life into Glassboro, but it resulted in the creation of an engineering school and a name change from Glassboro State College to Rowan College of New Jersey (recently changed again to Rowan University in April 1997).

Who is this man, who, in one fell swoop, surpassed the Rockefellers, Vanderbilts, and Astors? His autobiography, entitled *The Fire Within*, reveals a simple man who is more in touch with his South Jersey roots than the world of high finance and industry. "I spend time with people because I like them," he says. "Being wealthier than the next guy may be important to some, but it means little to me. I enjoy doing what I do." As a result, Rowan has never been interested in hobnobbing with society's elite.

The third child of Dr. Henry M. Rowan Sr. and Margaret Frances Boyd Rowan, he was born in 1923. Two events profoundly shaped his youth: the stock market crash in 1929, in which his family lost its fortune, and his parent's divorce. His mother, a Wellesley College graduate, tried to be both mother and father to him. On one occasion, she took Rowan and his brother out of school for a month for a trip to Peru. Traveling in a banana boat, they lived like the seamen. When in Peru, they scaled the Andes and explored Inca ruins. At home, he started his first business when he was 9, raising chickens and selling eggs. His mother was his first customer. Not wanting to spoil him, she wouldn't pay more than the top wholesale price for eggs. To cut costs, young Rowan asked for a 100-lb. bag of feed for his birthday instead of a toy. He was a born entrepreneur.

Growing up in the Depression shaped much of his philosophy about wealth. He considers waste to be sinful, and still drives a 1990 Buick. The fact that he flies a Lear jet is not a contradiction. "The Lear is a business tool, a real profit earner," he says. Rowan either flies customers to one of his plants or sends troubleshooters to handle customer problems.

141

A graduate of MIT and a World War II veteran, Rowan started Inductotherm Industries, Inc. in Rancocas, Burlington County, in 1954. For start-up capital, Rowan sold the family home. Rowan and his wife built their first furnace in their cellar, heating the copper over a bonfire in their backyard. Today, Inductotherm Industries, Inc. is a world leader in the manufacture of induction melting furnaces and related products. The company has grown to include 80 subsidiaries located in North America, South America, Europe, India, Asia, and Australia.

Despite his wealth, he has not led a charmed life. Like the rest of us, he worked hard for what he has. He has even faced tragedy: the death of two sons from a rare muscle disease. Both died in their 20s. Rowan credits his wife for caring for the boys. "That Betty had kept both alive so long in the face of a disease that permitted few victims to survive beyond their teens is remarkable," he says. His daughter, Virginia Smith, lives in Moorestown. Although Rowan is pleased with his gift, which is administered by a foundation, he says that his normal business activities have made a greater contribution in the South Jersey area. Over the years, he has paid out $3 billion in salaries and expenditures locally. South Jersey has always been short of great natural resources, but never short of inventive people, as the story of Henry Rowan shows.

Photo of Henry Rowan is courtesy of Rowan University in Glassboro.

Index

Vixen Laura, 43-44
Vuotto family, 80

W

Waas, J. C., 118
wages, 80
Walczak, Tom, 138
Wanagrams, 104
Wanamaker, John, xii, 102-104
Warner, Edmund, 11
Washington, George, 39-40
Washington, Isaac, 134
Washington, Sara Spenser, xii, 133-134
weather, 120-121
weaving, 40
Webb, Pegleg John, 99-100
Webster, Daniel, 62
Welch, Charles, 89-90
Welch, Thomas, xiii, 89-91, *91*
Wells, Rachel Lovell, 55
Wentzel, Johannis, 17
Wesley, John, 55
whaling, 53
Wharton, Joseph, 110
Wheaton, T. C., 107-108
Wheaton Industries, 108
Whilden, Hannah, 53-54
White, Elizabeth, xiii, 116-117, *117*

White Horse Pike, 97
Whitesbog, 116
Williams, Carl, 59
Willow, Angelina, 83
Wills Island, 6
Wilson, President Woodrow, 106
Wilted Grass, Chief, 6, 97
Wimberg, Henry, 112
Winder, Captain, 69
wines, 66
Wistar, Caspar, xiii, 17-18
Wolsieffer, Phillip Mathias, 77-78, *78*
women. *See also* Moravian Sisterhood;
    Wright, Patience Lovell
    Antoinette Doell, 129-131, *130*
    Indian Ann, 97-98
    voting rights, 42
    and War of Independence, 40-42
    Washington, Sara Spenser, xii, 133-134
Wood, Margaretta, 36
Woolman, John, 32-34, *33*
World War I, 134
World War II, 130
Wright, Patience Lovell, xi, xii, 55-56

Z

Zion Methodist Church, 31

For
Further Reading

I am indebted to the following fine authors and historians for their research and insights. For more information on the people and times chronicled in this book, order these books or articles from your local library.

Books

Bakeless, John and Katherine. *Signers of the Declaration.* Boston: Houghton Mifflin Co. 1969.

Cunningham, Barbara. *The New Jersey Ethnic Experience.* Union City, NJ: Wm. H. Wise and Co. 1977.

Cunningham, John T. *New Jersey: America's Main Road.* Garden City, NY: Doubleday and Company. 1966.

Cunz, Dieter. *Egg Harbor City: New Germany in New Jersey.* N. P. 1956.

Fowler, Michael, and Herbert, William. *Papertown of the Pine Barrens.* Eatontown, NJ: Environmental Education Publishing Service. 1976.

Green, Charles F. *Pleasant Mills, New Jersey; Lake Nescochague, A Place of Olden Days.* N. P.

Kross, Peter. *New Jersey History.* Wilmington, DE: The Middle Atlantic Press. 1987.

McCormick, Richard P. *New Jersey from Colony to State: 1609-1789.* Princeton, NJ: D. Van Nostrand Co., Inc. 1986.

McMahon, William. *Pine Barrens Legend, Lore, and Lies.* Wilmington, DE: The Middle Atlantic Press. 1980.

McMahon, William. *South Jersey Towns: History and Legend.* New Brunswick, NJ: Rutgers University Press. 1973.

McMahon, William. *The Story of Hammonton*. Hammonton, NJ: The Historical Society of Hammonton. 1960.

Moonsammy, et al. *Pinelands Folklife*. New Brunswick, NJ: Rutgers University Press. 1987.

Palmer, F. Alan. *This Place Called Home*. Upper Deerfield Township, NJ: 1985.

Pierce, Arthur D. *Family Empire in Jersey Iron*. New Brunswick, NJ: Rutgers University Press. 1964.

Rundstrom, Olive Conover. *History of Somers Point*. Atlantic County Historical Society. 1968.

Studley, Miriam V. *Historic New Jersey Through Visitors' Eyes*. Princeton, NJ: D. Van Nostrand Co., Inc. 1964.

Weiss, Harry B. *Life in Early New Jersey*. Princeton, NJ: D. Van Nostrand Co., Inc. 1964.

Wilbur, H. W., and Hand, W. B. *Illustrated History of the Town of Hammonton*. Hammonton, NJ: The Mirror Steam Printing House. 1889.

Articles

Chestnut, Bill. "The Inventive Mind of Henry Hettinger." *South Jersey Magazine*. (Spring, 1989): 17.

Goldy, James. "Cornelia Hancock: Angel of Mercy." *South Jersey Magazine*. (Winter, 1985): 24-28.

Perinchief, Elizabeth. "David and John Brainerd: Missionaries in the Pines." *Batsto Citizens Gazette*. (Spring and Summer, 1977): 5.